GW00787521

c

Hello,

Congratulations on picking up this guide to Facebook. Whether you are a complete newcomer to the world of social networking, or an old hand, we promise you will learn something useful. Facebook is the fastest-growing social networking site in the world, and, for many people, has become the hub of their online friendships.

Which means that it's not just about having a profile, it's about making that profile work harder for you. But don't worry, we're here to show you exactly how to do that.

Are you ready to effortlessly become a Facebook expert? Then carry on reading…

In this guide you'll find out how to:
- *Create a brighter, better homepage*
- *Make new friends, and find old ones*
- *Meet celebrities online*
- *Take a great profile picture*
- *Upload videos*
- *Be safe online*
- *Hold successful real-life events*
- *And much, much, much more*

We'll also be showing the best Facebook profile pictures we've found in our galleries, sharing amazing tips about the best games on the site, and helping you get the most of your online experience. Have fun! ■

The independent guide to Facebook

EDITORIAL
Editor David McComb
Managing Editor Simon Clays
Features Editor Kate Hodges
Chief Sub Editor Greg Hughes

ART
Art Director Russell Clark
Art Editor Mike Mansfield
Picture Editor Tom Broadbent

COVER PHOTO
Getty Images

CONTRIBUTORS
Photos: Joe Plimmer, Tom Broadbent
Words: Chris Bourn, Tom Broadbent, James Doorne, Simon Edwards, Isla Harvey, Sharon O'Dea, Sarah Rabia, Amy Salter, Denise Stanborough, Alex Watson

DENNIS PUBLISHING CONSUMER DIVISION:
Group Publishing Director Simon Clark
Managing Director Bruce Sandell

DENNIS PUBLISHING LIMITED
Chief Operating Officer Brett Reynolds
Chief Executive James Tye
Executive Director Kerin O'Connor
Group Finance Director Ian Leggit
Chairman Felix Dennis

Printing benhamgoodhead print Ltd

Origination/retouching
Darren Brooke and Dave Kinnard (Mullis Morgan)

Dennis Publishing
30 Cleveland Street, London W1T 4JD
Tel: (020) 7907 6000

This way

The independent guide to

Facebook

Famous on
Facebook
62

Taking a
Good Picture
32

Photos: Rex Features and Corbis

Guides and help

Walkthrough
We'll take you
through everything
you need to know,
step by step

Learn stuff
Did you know that
a Facebook group
of 74 people think
'David Cameron is
a Hottie'?

Who's the funniest actor in the world? **p128**

Facebook in the News108

Galleries

This way

Face facts

Between one million and two million people are on Facebook simultaneously at any given time of the day or night.

Why Facebook?

If you're not on Facebook, you will be soon. All your friends are already there. And they're probably talking about you, posting pictures of you, and establishing campaigns to get you to to sign up as a user. Believe us

Words **Kate Hodges**

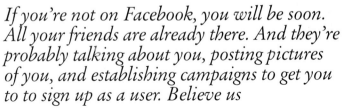

This way

stablished by Mark Zuckerberg in 2004 as a Harvard University social site, by October 2007, the social networking site had 50million users around the world. In that month, Microsoft invested £117m in exchange for a mere 1.6% share of the company. It's a huge success story, but what makes it so massively popular? And why should you make sure that you're not only part of it, but that you know how to get the best out of the site?

The concept of Facebook is simple. Members have their own profile, which they can update with pictures and videos. They can add 'applications' – add-ons that let them do specific fun things like playing 'Pacman' or showing off the books they've read. And they can stay in touch with friends via personal messages, join groups to meet like-minded people, and find new friends. And, because of the site's innovative open structure, members are constantly developing new functions to play with.

Facebook is a neverending reality show, and you and your friends are the stars at the centre of it

So just why has Facebook exploded in popularity? First, it's easy to use and free to join. It's funded by advertising, and by selling data. So unlike sites such as Friends Reunited, you won't have to pay to contact your friends, or to upload your videos and your pictures.

Second, it's addictive. It's not earned the name 'crackbook' for nothing. Applications encourage you to revisit. To play your turn against your friend at 'Scrabulous', an online, Facebook-hosted version

of Scrabble, to reply to an urgent message someone you really fancy has sent you, to check out the photos of your friend's wedding they've uploaded.

Unlike many websites, since you interact with Facebook, you and your friends create the content that keeps you all coming back. From minute-by-minute status reports to shaky cameraphone videos of concerts, there's always something new to gawp at on Facebook, and it's always starring your friends. It's a neverending reality show you're the centre of. Babies, jobs, weddings, parties. The addictiveness of Facebook comes not from the technology itself, but from the people, the stories, and the pictures it streams to you constantly.

In our time-poor, globally scattered society, many people find they don't have time to stay in contact with friends, either face-to-face or by phone. So Facebook acts as a way to keep up with mates and family when you are free. You catch up with news when you want, rather than relying on two busy people being free to speak at the same time.

▲ CRACKBOOK is one of the nicknames that have been handed to the super-addictive social website

---

A brief history of Facebook

The meteoric rise of a $15billion phenomenon

● **14 May 1984**
Facebook creator Mark Zuckerberg born in Westchester County, New York.

● **2002**
Zuckerberg enrols at Harvard University.

● **2004**
Microsoft founder Bill Gates speaks at Harvard. Zuckerberg attends and is inspired. He says, "He really encouraged all of us to take time off school to work on a project. That's a policy at Harvard – you can take as much time off as you want."

● **4 February 2004**
Facebook officially founded. It's first called 'The Facebook'.

● **September 2004**
Facebook receives around $500,000 in a donation from PayPal co-founder Peter Thiel.

● **December 2004**
Facebook signs up its millionth member.

Facebook also encourages sheer bloody-minded competitiveness. Dr Will Reader and his team at Sheffield Hallam university have been investigating online friendships. They claim Facebook and similar sites can attract competitive 'friending', where people "collect friends like boys collect Airfix models". They have also observed that people collect 'trophy friends' – famous people, sexy girls, or bands.

Others use the site as a way to get in touch with long-lost friends from school. Unlike a potentially rejectable email, a Facebook 'poke' is a cheeky and informal way of getting in touch with an old crush, a long-lost friend, or even a beloved ex-teacher.

Of course, there are plenty of other networking sites, but Facebook is, at the moment, growing the fastest. Unlike the other huge social networking site, MySpace, your Facebook profile is impossible (at

▲ FACEBOOK HQ in Palo Alto, California, caters to its young pool of employees with a creative, dorm-like atmosphere

Huge numbers of people now have Facebook set as their homepage. For them, it IS the internet

the moment) to 'customise'. So the glittery graphics like something from a three-year-old's birthday card that infest MySpace are missing, as are the flashy backgrounds that make any writing on top of them impossible to read. Facebook is all cool blue and soothing white, and profiles are easy to navigate.

MySpace has attempted to win back the hordes stampeding from it in the direction of Facebook by emulating Facebook's clean design lines and status updates in a rejig. But, just as users migrated from fledging social site Friendster towards MySpace

when it first became popular, so those same fickle users are now flocking to Facebook. Because of the site's origins in the collegiate world, it has (rightly or wrongly) more of a reputation for being popular with those higher up the social and academic ladder. It also has more older users than other networking sites. It's a more adult place to hang out online, where friendships are worked on, and new relationships (personal, academic, and professional) are forged.

Such is the impact of the site, that huge numbers of people now have Facebook set as their homepage. For them, it IS the internet – the place they meet their friends, catch up on gossip, and see and hear what their friends have been up to. A working knowledge of the site is essential, but an in-depth appreciation of how to use Facebook to your full advantage is even better. Lucky then, that you have this book in your hands. ■

● **May 2005**
Facebook raises $12.7million from venture capitalists Accel Partners.

● **2005**
Zuckerberg drops out of college.

● **August 2005**
Site is overhauled to make it more user-friendly, and switches domain to Facebook.com, dropping the unwieldy 'the' from its original title.

Why did the UK fall in love with Facebook?

By internet psychologist **Graham Jones**

"Facebook users know they can send each other little messages, even buy their 'friends' an online drink or send them a 'hug'. You can even do all that with text messages, sending little 'wordlets'. But there's a more subtle connection, a psychological one.

Written language is used when we can't see or hear each other. For millions of years, humans and their forebears have used coding systems, like written language, to pass on information. Early cave paintings were codes for where to find food, for instance.

A million years of social networking

However, if you were next to your cave mate, you didn't need a painting, you could tell them caveman to caveman where the best hunting was. So, spoken language is for when we are with people, written language is for when we aren't together. Our brains are built that way – we know the difference and use written language or spoken language appropriately.

Most voicemails don't get messages left on them. People put the phone down. Why? Because they know they're speaking to no-one; that's just stupid. When no-one's there we write to them – hey presto, texting.

So what's this got to do with Facebook? Well, writing messages on our friend's 'Fun Wall' is great when we are not together. We can write to them because they are not with us. Perfect. Even more perfect for us Brits.

● **2 September 2005**
The high-school version of Facebook launched.

● **11 December 2005**
Universities in Australia and New Zealand are added to the Facebook network.

● **February 24, 2006**
Two users hack the site to make infected profiles look like MySpace. The culprits are later employed by Facebook.

● **11 September 2006**
Facebook made available to any user with a valid email address.

● **September 2006**
Yahoo! reportedly makes an offer of nearly $1billion for the social network.

British reserve

We don't like admitting it – after all we're a bit reserved – but the rest of the world knows that on the whole British people are not that sociable. In fact, we'd often rather be quiet, on our own, or only with true friends.

But walk into a bar in the USA, and before you know it six people have started talking to you, and you know all about their grandchildren and their plans to become a millionaire. The Americans live in an environment where talking to real people is encouraged. We don't – what do we tell our children at school? Be quiet. Don't talk. We are brought up to avoid spoken language. Guess what that means?

It means things like texting and sending people pretend hugs and drinks is much more attractive to British people than those hug-loving French, for instance. So, it's no surprise that two pieces of research show just how much the people in the UK love technologically based socialising because it allows us to avoid the real thing.

A study of mobile-phone users across Europe has shown we are the text champions, SMS-ing much more than our European cousins and way, way more than people in the USA.

Brits spend more time than any other country in Europe using Facebook. That's because they are all out at dinner parties and in bars and restaurants with their friends, while we are nice and safely tucked up, on our own, behind our computer screens.
Grahamjones.co.uk

● **10 May 2007,** Facebook adds free classified adverts to the website.

● **24 May 2007** Launches the Facebook Platform, a means for developers to create their own applications.

● **2007** Zuckerberg tells *Forbes* magazine, "I didn't care about being a CEO and I never really have, I didn't even care about running a company – I just wanted to build cool things."

● **24 October 2007** Microsoft pays $240million (£117million) for a 1.6% stake.

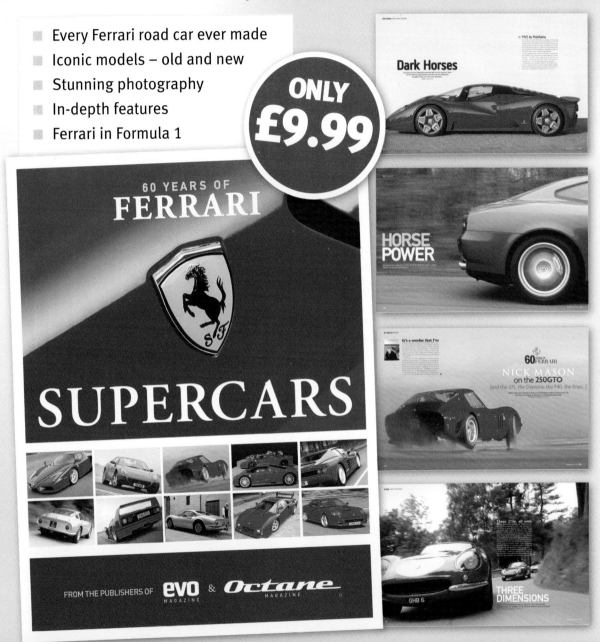

Gallery party

What's the point of having a great night out if you can't share it with your friends the morning after? Facebook is the perfect place to show off and share last night's party snaps.

Andy
This is me and the boys on holiday in Asturias, Spain. Five days of non-stop partying, surfing, food and table football!

Dan
Me and my mate Mango getting trolleyed at his stag do. It was a big night, and I felt a little worse for wear the next morning!

Jo
Because two drinks are always better than one!

Rob
Starting 'em early! Our daytrip to France turned nasty when toddler Rob decided now was the time to start drinking litre glasses of beer!

Andy
Taken in a small bar in Hollywood, me and the Turkish Prince knocking back a couple

Carlovely
Classy – swigging mouthwash. This picture was taken in my bathroom at 4am

Jenni
No particular reason why I took this, just enjoying the greatness that is the Jager!

James
This picture was taken by renowned Belfast photographer Iona Bateman – and that's her I'm spitting on!

Next Gallery
Awwwww! What better way to show off your darling offspring than on your Facebook page?
p30

Face facts

In October 2007, Facebook had 42million users worldwide. Over 60million users are hoped for by the end of the year.

Getting started

Setting up a Facebook profile is simple, and it won't be long before you're chatting online and tracking down long-lost friends. Here's how to get started, with some valuable tips for experts and newbies alike…

Words **Sharon O'Dea**

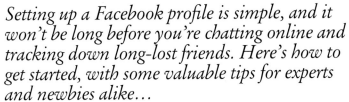
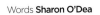

This way

1 "How do I register for Facebook?"

◄ THE VERY first screen you'll see when you arrive at Facebook

First, go to Facebook.com and click on 'Sign Up'. You'll be taken to a registration page, where you enter your name, work status, and email address. It's vital you use an email address you check regularly, as Facebook will contact you for confirmation of registration, and will send regular email notifications of profile updates. Next, enter a password and your birthday, type the security prompt, then agree to the terms and conditions. Now just click 'Sign Up Now' and a confirmation email will be sent to the address you entered. Log on to your email, click on the link provided by Facebook, and you'll go directly to your new profile.

Quick tip! When entering your email details, don't use a work address if possible. Many employers take a dim view of employees viewing Facebook profiles during work hours, and regular email updates to your company inbox could potentially get you in trouble!

◄ ENTER your details and type in the letters to get past the spam filter

2 "How do I find my best friends?"

◄ THAT'S IT! You are now officially on Facebook

Now you're set up, it's time to personalise your profile and fill your list of friends. After confirming registration, Facebook will offer to search your web-based email address book for friends who are already members, and all you have to do is enter your email address and password (this will not work with all email providers, however, and while users of Hotmail, Yahoo, Gmail and AOL won't have problems, some may require you to add addresses manually). When presented with a list of friends, pick the ones to add by ticking the boxes, then click 'Add To Friends' at the bottom.

Quick tip! Having a large group of Facebook friends will make you look well-connected and popular, but do you really want to be in touch with people you haven't spoken to for years? If you're not in contact with someone already, there's probably a good reason for that!

◄ THE SITE can now search for Facebook friends using your email address

3 "What are networks all about?"

After entering details of where you live, the company you work for and the name of your old school, you'll be asked to join a regional network, which will be based on the information you've already entered. You cannot view people's Facebook profiles unless you're friends with each other, but you can look at anyone's if you're both in the same network. Once you've completed this stage, you'll be taken to your blank profile – and if other people from your workplace are members of Facebook, you'll be offered a list of colleagues you can choose to add. Or ignore!

◀ FILL IN your work, school and location info

◀ SET YOUR Network. This could be your region, or your work, for instance

Quick tip! Users who don't want other regional network members to view their profile can adjust Facebook's privacy settings to suit their tastes. For more details on using Facebook's privacy settings, see p72.

Your questions...

"*What is my status update?*" Becks from Peckham

Like a micro-blog, your 'status update' (found on the right-hand side of your profile) is a great way to keep your friends up-to-date on your feelings or what you're doing, using only a handful of words. Sadly, the status update follows the annoying '[Your name] is...' format, which can make it hard to phrase comments in the way you want. In fact, many groups have been founded on Facebook to complain about this, most notably the 'Take Away the Mandatory "is" Before the Status' group.

"*What is poking all about?*" Jason from Hackney

If you want to say hello to one of your friends, but you can't be bothered writing them a proper email or scribbling on their Facebook wall, 'poking' is the ideal way to get their attention. When they next log on to Facebook, they'll see a message that you poked them, and can either choose to ignore you or poke back. Once you start poking, it's hard to stop – in fact, poking sessions can last for years as prompts are bounced back and forth!

4 "How do friends contact me?"

Next, click on 'Contact'. Here you can add a screen name that people will see when they view your profile, and you can also, if you wish, enter your phone number, address and the area where you live. If you have your own website, you can also list the URL. When you're happy, select 'Save Changes', then click on 'Relationships' to load a page where you can enter more details on your love life, the name of your partner, and the reason you've become a member of Facebook. If you're single and feeling lucky, tick the 'Whatever I Can Get' box and see if love comes your way!

> **Quick tip!** When entering personal information, it's set up in such a way that only your Facebook friends will be able to view the details. However, if you're nervous about personal info appearing on the site, try playing around with the privacy settings (see p79).

◄ENTER your contact details if you like – you may prefer to leave some parts blank

◄YOU CAN mention your better half – or your singledom!

5 "How do I add my personality?"

The next step is to click on 'Personal'. This is where you can make your Facebook profile reflect your personality and shout about the things you love, including your favourite music, TV shows, books, quotes and so on. Make sure you click 'Save Changes' when you're done, otherwise you'll lose all the information you spent hours sweating over.

> **Quick tip!** The boxes where you enter this information can hold a lot of text, and many users are tempted to include every single song, film or book they've ever enjoyed. But the more text people are presented with, the less likely they are to read it! So keep the personal details short and interesting, and only include the things you truly adore.

◄FILL IN some details about your personality and interests

◄DON'T go overboard on details, though, as it can clog up your profile

6 "How do I start adding details?"

Now you're established on Facebook, it's time to personalise your profile. If you click on 'Profile' in the blue bar at the top of the page you'll see all the sections are empty, so click 'Edit' and you'll be asked to enter personal details. First, click on 'Basic' and enter your sex, whether you're interested in men or women, your relationship status, and what sort of friendships you're seeking on Facebook. Next, select your birthday, hometown, and describe your religious views. Once you're happy, click 'Save Changes'.

▲ UPDATE your status, when you're ready

▲ POLITICAL views can be shared too – or not!

Quick tip! Don't worry if you enter the wrong info or make spelling mistakes – you can always go back and edit your details by following the same routine detailed above. And you don't have to fill in anything you don't want to; if you're uncomfortable talking about your religious views, or you don't think your politics are anyone else's business, just leave the boxes blank.

How to make friends

Always bear in mind that having hundreds of friends doesn't automatically make you look cool. In fact, it can make you look desperate, as if you don't have any real friends. But if you're determined to boost your friend list, here are a few common strategies...

Steal friends
■ The most common way to increase your number of Facebook mates is to view your friends' lists and add their contacts. This can often lead to resentment – especially if you start stealing people you don't know – but it's the easiest way to find casual acquaintances and likeminded folk.

Befriend strangers
■ It's not a popular practice – and most Facebookers will choose to ignore friend requests from people they don't know – but trying to add strangers is an effective way to boost your list. To make the process easier, join groups where you'll find people who like the same sorts of things, with whom you'll at least have something in common.

Have a great profile
■ If there's one thing guaranteed to prompt strangers to try to 'friend' you, it's a great Facebook profile. If you have a striking portrait, you'll soon find that everyone who stumbles across your profile online will want to be your friend, making it even more important that you read our photo advice on p32.

Invite new people
■ If you search for a friend and they're not a member of Facebook, you can enter their email address and invite them to join. Asking loads of people who haven't taken the Facebook plunge is a good way to boost your list, but don't be surprised if most people ignore this unsolicited invitation.

7 "How do I find my old school pals?"

◀ ADDING your school details can help old school pals find you

Click on 'Education' and you'll be able to enter more details about your current or former school or college, and the year you graduated. This will help other people from your school find you, and you can also use the 'Find Former High School Classmates' and 'Find Current Or Past University Classmates' links at the bottom of the page to look for long-lost buddies. Just remember, though, people change over the years, and may not be the 'best friend ever' you remember...

◀ BUT MANY prefer to leave their school details blank. Were they really the 'good old days'?

Quick tip! Many people look back at their school days with rose-tinted glasses – but in reality they were probably some of the worst times of your life! It might be fun to find out what the school bully or your first love are up to these days, but are you ready to be pestered by tedious emails about the 'good old days' and invitations to attend class reunions? Thought not!

8 "How do I find my work colleagues?"

◀ THE SAME applies to your place of work

Click on 'Work' and you'll be able to expand on the employment details you've already entered. As well as the name of the company you work for, you can display a description of what your job involves, and the length of time you've worked there. And if you didn't do so when you first logged on to your new Facebook account, you can use the 'Find Coworkers...' link at the bottom of the page to locate and add your colleagues to your friends.

◀ MAKE sure you're not too candid about your working conditions

Quick tip! There's a big temptation when filling out this page to be cynical about your low pay and appalling working conditions – but the joke might backfire if your boss sees your profile! Remember, you don't have to fill out every detail, so if you want to be friends with your work colleagues, don't take any risks – leave the 'Position' and 'Description' boxes blank.

Face facts

There are over 47,000 Facebook groups. Meanwhile, there are over 5,600 applications for users of the site to download, and in the real world, the company employs in excess of 300 people. Not bad for three Harvard students who set the site up from their dorm room.

9 "How do I add a profile picture?"

Now all the text details are entered, it's time to click on 'Picture' and add an image that'll become your online 'face'. Don't worry, you can change this photo any time you like. On this page you'll also see a 'thumbnail' of your profile picture that will be used in other parts of Facebook. Remember to be careful about the picture you use; would your employer or college get angry if they saw the pic? Is there anything going on in the background that's illegal or immoral? Does the picture make you look like an idiot? Think carefully before uploading.

Quick tip! When uploading pictures you can only use Jpg, Gif or Png image files, so you may need to convert your picture beforehand so it's in one of these formats. Don't leave your profile pic as Facebook's big blue question mark! It's ugly, and makes it harder for people to find you.

◄ PROFILES can look a little blank without a photo added

◄ THIS IS the shot that will show up on a search, so make sure you pick the right one

10 "Can I change my profile layout?"

While the options for changing the appearance of your Facebook page are limited when compared to other social networking sites such as MySpace, you have some control over your profile layout. Simply use your mouse to click on, drag and drop boxes of info around your profile, and Facebook will let you know if you can make the adjustments. Unfortunately, you can't move your 'Mini-Feed' or 'Friends' boxes, and some info may be restricted to the left or right column of your profile. To make any changes to the layout, just click on 'Profile' at the top of the page and start dragging.

Quick tip! If you're determined to change the way your profile looks, some whizzkids have written programmes that allow you to do this. We don't have time to cover these programmes here, but a quick Google search should reveal the details you need.

◄ WHY NOT personalise the look of your profile?

◄ BOXES and your applications can be laid out to your own taste

11 "How can I find more friends"

◀ SEARCH for friends by name using the basic search function

Now your profile is set up, you can start looking for more friends. First, click on 'Friends' in the blue bar at the top of your profile, and if you haven't done so already you'll be given the option to search your web-based email address book, as well as search for people who match your school, college and work details. Click on the 'Contact Us' link if you're having problems with this and Facebook will email you back with advice. In the 'Search' bar on the left-hand side of every page, you can also browse for specific names.

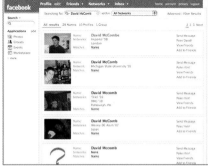

◀ DON'T BE surprised if you come up with multiple similar results, however!

Quick tip! When you make someone your friend, you're given the option to enter details of how you know them, when you met and so on. It might seem a chore to enter this info time and again, but Facebook can take this data and make a 'social timeline' – a fascinating way to see how various people came into your life over the years. Just click 'Social Timeline' in the 'Friends' area.

Your questions…

"What is my news feed?" Emma from Hornchurch

The centre of your Facebook profile includes the 'News Feed', which is designed to let you know what your friends are up to. Whether they've added a new application, accepted a new friend or changed their profile picture, you'll find out about it here first – whether you're interested or not. For most Facebook users, keeping an eye on their News Feed is what takes up most of their time online.

"What are events?" Nick from Liverpool

Click on the 'Events' link on the left-hand side of your profile and you'll get a reminder of any invitations you've accepted from other members and see which events your friends are attending. You can even create an event invitation for your friends, which is useful if you're arranging a party or big night out.

12 "Why should I join a network?"

To get a better idea of the scale of Facebook and the number of people using it, click on 'Networks' at the top of your profile. Here you'll be able to see how many people are in your regional network, browse member profiles, read posts, learn about upcoming events in your local area, and generally get to grips with the sprawling online community you've joined.

Quick tip! Had enough of your regional network? Then scroll to the bottom of the 'Network' page and click on the 'Leave This Network' link. You can then click on 'Network' again to choose another regional network, or go for a school or work one instead.

◄ YOU CAN find out what is going on in your area or workplace by joining a network

◄ ONCE you join up to a network, you can meet others with similar interests

13 "How do I add a photo library?"

One of the beauties of Facebook is that you can create online photo albums, which you can share with friends. To create a photo album, click on 'Photos', then click on the grey 'Create A Photo Album' button on the right. Enter the 'Name', 'Location' and 'Description' details, then choose who's allowed to view your album. The next page will allow you to find where the photos are on your hard drive, then they'll be uploaded into your profile. Afterwards you can choose to name your pictures and give viewers more details.

Quick tip! If there are several people in a photo you've just uploaded, follow the onscreen prompts and you'll be able to 'tag' individuals in the shot with a caption. If the person you've tagged is one of your Facebook friends, they'll get a message to let them know. But if they don't like what they see, they can easily 'untag' the picture!

◄ PHOTO galleries are one of the pleasures of Facebook

◄ CREATE albums of shots for your family and friends to enjoy

14 "How do I add mobile pics?"

While not everyone owns a digital camera, most people have access to a cameraphone – hence the proliferation of mobile snaps on Facebook. To make things easier, you can send phone pictures directly to your Facebook account. Simply click on the 'Photos' link and select 'Create Photo Album'. Click on the 'Mobile Photos' tag and you'll be asked to send a photo from your phone to Photos@facebook.com. Facebook will then send you back a code to confirm your phone number, and then you can send photos directly to your online profile.

Quick tip! Cameraphones are incredibly popular, but getting a decent snap from your mobile can be difficult. For tips on taking a decent shot with your phone, see p37.

◄ PHOTOS can also be posted on Facebook via your mobile

◄ A CODE IS sent by the site, you enter it, and photos are directly applied to your account

Staying in touch with Facebook

Facebook is all about being part of a community – so it's no surprise you can contact people in variety of ways.

Inbox

■ If you want to have a private exchange with one of your friends, you can send them a message, in much the same way as a traditional email. The good thing about messaging on Facebook is that you can view the whole conversation in sequence, rather than having to plough through your inbox to remind yourself how an argument kicked off...

Wall

■ If you want to send a message to someone and you don't care who sees it, scribble on their wall. Simply select your friend's profile, then scroll down until you see 'The Wall' and the white space to 'Write Something'. When you do, anyone who views the profile will see the message, and details of the exchange will appear in your 'News Feed'. You can even have 'wall to wall' exchanges this way.

Status update

■ To make sure everyone knows what you're up to, simply update your status with a few well-chosen words – these details will then appear in the 'Status Updates' box on the right-hand side of your profile.

◀ PRIVATE conversations can be carried out in much the same way as a normal email exchange

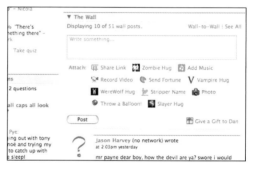

◀ MESSAGES that are for public consumption can be posted on your friend's wall

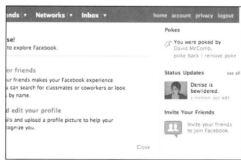

◀ STATUS updates keep your friends up to date with how you're feeling and how your day's going

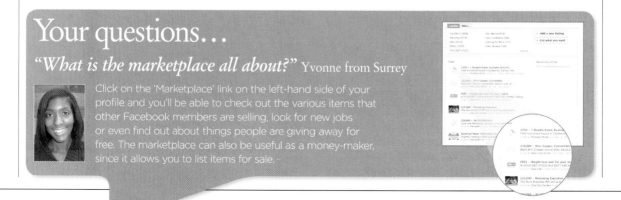

Your questions...

"What is the marketplace all about?" Yvonne from Surrey

Click on the 'Marketplace' link on the left-hand side of your profile and you'll be able to check out the various items that other Facebook members are selling, look for new jobs or even find out about things people are giving away for free. The marketplace can also be useful as a money-maker, since it allows you to list items for sale.

Facebook Etiquette

As Facebook is a sprawling online community, it's inevitable that some people will act in a way that annoys fellow members. Based on online blogs, articles and using Facebook religiously, here are our tips on Facebook etiquette.

Don't be scared to 'ignore'

● Probably the number-one conundrum on Facebook is how to respond when you're contacted by a blast from the past you don't particularly feel like getting back in touch with. Don't let this worry you – if you 'ignore' them when they friend request you (by pressing the 'Ignore' button), they won't get a message saying you rejected them, or anything awkward like that. It's just like pretending you didn't see someone on a bus – it happens to everyone.

Birthday greetings

● Facebook keeps a track of your friends' birthdays, and sending them a message on their special day only takes a second and will save your conscience for forgetting to send a card, so take the time to ping them off a message.

Friending stangers

● Although adding people you haven't met as friends is a good way to boost your list, it's a practice that's frowned upon by Facebook aficionados. They even have a name for these people: Creepers.

Stay sober

● Like drunken text messages, inebriated wall posts will only lead to heartache. Don't drink and Facebook.

Stay tidy

● There are thousands of Facebook applications to try, but having too many can clutter your profile and make you look like a geek. Remember that you can delete applications once you get bored with them, and there are often several applications to choose from that do the same thing (to check out the best applications, see the chapter starting p42).

Respect the wall

● There's nothing cool about opening your profile and finding some wag has drawn a naked woman on your wall made from asterisks, dollar signs and dashes. It's a public display to Facebook friends, so show some respect.

Avoid shrines

● There's nothing more tragic than a Facebook profile devoted to a loved one or potential partner. Facebook is all about *you* - not someone else you're trying to impress.

Adding Applications

So you're now a paid-up member of Facebook. Maybe it's time to add a few applications so you can have some fun with your friends. Check out our guide on **p42**

Gallery children

Facebook makes it easy to keep in touch with friends and share family pictures. Here are some of our favourite tots.

Eva
This is my daughter Niobe down in Brighton. And yes, she is named after the *Matrix* character

Matthew
This picture of my daugher Alice makes me laugh every time I look at it.

Betsy
The thing about going to Lima is that there are little urchin kids everywhere who make a living by looking cute and posing for photos. But if you don't give them enough, you'll get a mouthful of abuse – in English!

Tom
My two daughters get
a little over-excited

Robert
Taken on a daytrip
to London by Uncle Russ

Kate
I knew it was a bad
idea to buy my niece
Jeannie an ice cream

Tim
This is my son Harry and
me. He fancied a kip on my
shoulder after a busy night
of crying, feeding, crying
and, er, more feeding

Adrian
I went to a music festival,
and spotted this baby sipping
from a can of beer

Jaime
This is me and my daughter,
Hanifah, who's three-and-a-half. It was
taken around 6.30 in the morning.
We're both staring into the two-inch
screen on my old digital camera

Next
Gallery
Anyone can be an artist
with digital technology.
See some of our
favourite manipulations
p40

Face facts

Facebook is currently the number-one site on the web for sharing photographs, with 70,000 images served per second.

Your profile picture

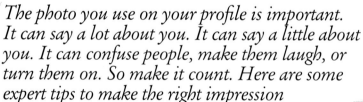

The photo you use on your profile is important. It can say a lot about you. It can say a little about you. It can confuse people, make them laugh, or turn them on. So make it count. Here are some expert tips to make the right impression

Words **Tom Broadbent**

This way ➜

Taking a basic portrait

What to use: Your digital camera. Or your cameraphone. You don't need swanky equipment to get good results. You could just switch to auto and snap away, but let's try out some tricks to get better results.

❶ With portraits, avoid using wide-angle lenses since they tend to be unflattering. And while that fish-eye lens seems cool at first, using one is a bit of a cliche. A longer lens – that is, setting your zoom to about 2x/3x – will give you better results.

❷ Most cameras will have a slight delay from when you take the picture to the camera actually recording the photo. It's only a fraction of a second, but enough to ruin a potentially classic photo. Hold the camera steady until the picture has appeared in the screen.

❸ If you're taking an action shot, such as someone playing sport or running, pre-focus by holding the 'shutter' button halfway down and pointing it at a spot where the person will pass in a few seconds. Then click all the way a moment before. It takes a lot of practice to get this one right.

❹ It's worth taking the highest-quality photos you can, so you can do what you like with them – print them out at a large size, or use them as a screensaver. So set your camera at the full megapixel and the highest-quality setting. If you're running out of space then buy a bigger memory card.

ANGLES ▶ are an important consideration when taking your Facebook photos

◀ FISH-EYE lenses (left) may seem cool, but a long lens (right) will give better results

❺ Shoot lots of pictures; the beauty of digital is that you can review them and delete as you go. Pick the 'decisive moment' from a selection.

❻ Think about where you're standing and what your subject is doing, Order them around until they get in the right position. Think about perspective, get a kid's-eye-view, crawl on the floor and shoot upwards. Stand on a chair or ladder and point down. Think about where you're pointing the camera. Having half a face in the bottom corner might say more than just a dull snap of someone's face.

▼ ACTION shots can be improved by semi-focusing on a spot, and waiting for the subject to arrive

Photos: Tom Broadbent

❼ The light is your friend. Natural daylight is normally the best lighting, but with a bit of thought you can usually turn most situations to your advantage.

❽ What are you trying to say? There is a message behind every photo. Think laterally. Hold up a sign saying how much you fancy Charley off *Big Brother* or how much you like playing Scrabble on rainy afternoons in Dartford. Wear a mask, dress up in your fancy dress, feather boas etc. Protect your identity if that is important to you.

❾ Think about locations, take shots outside in the street, in the local shopping centre, the barbers, on a mountaintop, in the woods, at your office.

❿ Finally, your pictures don't have to be shots of you, they can be anything you want them to be. So a sunset might represent you better. Or your collection of rare vinyl records.

Shooting outside

▲ WHY NOT represent yourself in a creative way, like your author Tom Broadbent…

❶ Think about where you're standing and what the sun is doing, if there is any.

❷ Generally, if it's a sunny day, the best time to shoot is late afternoon, when the sun will be softer. Also, as a rule, it's best to shoot with the sun behind you.

◀ GIVE SOME thought to where you're standing in relation to the sun, or introduce some flash

❸ Check where your subject is standing or sitting. If they are under something like a tree they will be in shadow. Make sure you bring them out of it.

❹ Or if it's a perfect position but dark, introduce some flash to brighten things up. This is called fill-in, and you should find it on the flash settings, it will be the one where the flash symbol is highlighted.

❺ But it can be fun to shoot into the sun as well. Get your friend to stand so that they obscure the sun. Then shift to one side – you'll get all the sun's rays hitting your lens. Remember to not look directly at the sun. You need to focus on the person, hold the shutter button halfway down and let the sun in by moving your camera. A lovely crazy scene. You can also add flash using the technique described above.

SHOOTING ▶ into the sun can be fun. Adding flash can enhance your pictures

Night shooting

Bear in mind that the flash on a normal camera is only any good up to about 3m distance from the subject. Any further than that and it's pointless.
But if you shoot at night, you want to get a bit more creative than just snapping away with flash.

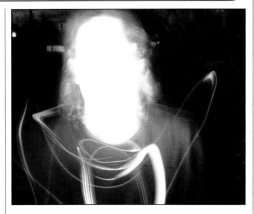

1 A good idea is to find an alternative light source. Why not try standing under a bus shelter, or using the light from a telephone box or at a railway station. Beware, though – with some of these situations, although you can see pretty clearly, the camera will struggle.

2 Try jamming the camera up against something solid, like a post, or rest it on top of a bench. Then set the camera to the night mode or use the fill-in flash as detailed on p35.

3 Try other light sources, such as torches or sparklers, to light the photo. Get the camera

◄ GLASS ►
and flash do not mix. Turn it off, otherwise you'll get reflections

◄ TORCHES can provide some interesting effects when used at night

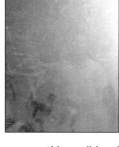 

on something solid and select night shooting. Put it on self-timer and hit the button.

4 Remember, if you're shooting anywhere where you're against glass, you won't be able to shoot with flash. Turn it off. Otherwise you'll get reflections.

5 Try to avoid red-eye. You can, of course, use the red-eye setting on the flash. A much more simple way of avoiding it is to simply point the camera at a slight angle to the person's face when you take a straight-on portrait.

Shooting inside

1 Stand next to a window – the natural light will be more flattering than the artificial light in the room.

2 No windows? Pull up the settings and select 'white balance'. This will make the photos look a lot more like a scene appears to the naked eye.

NATURAL ► light is the most flattering for your photos

◄ USING alternative light sources can offer interesting results at night

❸ Hit the film speed (ISO) button and stick it on 400. Now you can shoot with a mixture of available light and flash. Find the flash setting that says either 'slow sync' or has a flash symbol crossed, with an 'S'. Hold the camera steady or rest it on something solid. Now you'll get a softer effect with the flash.

❹ The professionals are always looking for ways to soften the lighting on portraits. Try using a piece of Scotchlite tape over your flash to soften it. Experiment with more layers of tape.

❺ If you're inside a dark building and your subject is more than 3m away, switch the flash off, stick the camera on something vaguely solid. And hope for the best!

❻ Introduce props like fairy lights, or stick some coloured paper over lights – anglepoise lamps are particularly good for this. Extra colours in the photos will brighten them up.

❼ Think about silhouettes. Get an overhead projector and make animals in the light, or stick your head in there. Turn off the flash and get interesting snaps of the shadow.

▲ INTRODUCE props like masks or toys to make your shots more exciting and fun

Using your mobile phone to shoot

Mobiles usually have more basic cameras, but with a few tricks, you'll still get great images

Always use good light
■ Even the most modern mobile-phone cameras will struggle in low light. You'll end up with really grainy, rough snaps.

Keep your subject still
■ Most phones have a long delay in taking the photo. So make sure the person holds their position until you have the result on your screen.

Keep it simple
■ Think of photos which will have an impact. After all, they're not going to be very big.

High quality
■ Set the phone to the highest-quality setting and get a bigger memory card so you don't run out of space.

Avoid using the zoom
■ Avoid using the zoom on the phone. They tend to be low quality. You're far better off getting closer.

Get intimate
■ As Eve Arnold (the famous Magnum photojournalist) once said, "You can never get too close." Don't be scared to get intimate with your subject.

Take extra photos
■ Take extra photos – you can always delete the ones which don't work.

Have fun
■ Finally, have fun – you can shoot lots of things with a phone, since you're always going to have it with you.

Tips from the professionals

If you want your shots to make an impact on Facebook you don't necessarily need snazzy equipment. Here's some advice from four world-famous lensmen

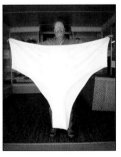

Jonathan Worth

Jonathan Worth is based in London and New York. He has photographed Billy Bob Thornton, The Killers and Christopher Lee, and has worked for *Rolling Stone*, *The Observer* and *Vogue*.
See his work at Jonathanworth.com

● Be aware of the light. Put your hand up to catch the light in it and see what your skin looks like. If it's a shaft of direct sunlight and the skin on your hand looks bleached out, move it to the reflected light at the side and see what it looks like there.
● A wide-angle lens will make you look as if you're on the back of a spoon (comedy value) if your camera has a zoom on it. A longer lens will be more flattering.
● Be conscious of the frame edges. Photography is as much about what you leave out as what you keep in.

Dario Rumbo

Dario Rumbo is a portrait and still-life photographer based in Barcelona. Recent pictures include commercials for Hewlett Packard and Bacardi, as well as a series of portraits of his family.
See his work at Dariorumbo.com

● Be out of focus to have a look that is 'you' but 'not you'. A resemblance, I will say.
● Using a simple background works best so there is just the attention on the face and no noise or distractions. Use both a dark and a light one to see what works best.
● Make it terrific!!!!! Use lighting in a dramatic way from underneath – a candle or a torch and a mirror is perfect for this – to take a self portrait that makes you go AHHHHHHH! Especially suitable for Halloween.

Dean Chalkley

Dean Chalkley has won many awards for his photography and has shot everyone from Arctic Monkeys to Oasis to The White Stripes. He's also produced fashion shoots for, among others, Levi's.
See his work at Deanchalkley.com

● Get a good simple idea of who you want to be... how do you see yourself? This is where it can get really interesting. How would you like to see yourself? A superhero? A clown? One half of a pantomine horse? You can be who you want to be, so go crazy.
● Don't get hung up on tech things. Facebook operates at low resolution, so as long as the camera renders a fairly accurate image of you that's all that counts – concentrate more on shooting loads!
● Have fun... take your camera wherever you go, and find funny, weird, abstract surroundings for your shots.

Neville Elder

Neville Elder is a photojournalist based in New York. He is as happy photographing celebrities as getting down and dirty shooting reportage features all over the world.
See his work at Nevilleelder.com

● Remember, the first Facebook picture people see of you is a thumbnail, so when taking it, place the subject to the edges of the frame, so it's just a face.
● Use good, even, natural light (not too sunny and not under striplights or indoor lighting). You can use flash.
● Have someone else take the picture for you – too many photos are taken on webcams or at arm's length, which looks horrible.
● When shooting, point down on the person from above (it's more flattering) and don't use a wide angle – a portrait is better on a longer lens.

Learn how to use Facebook groups – p118 ➡

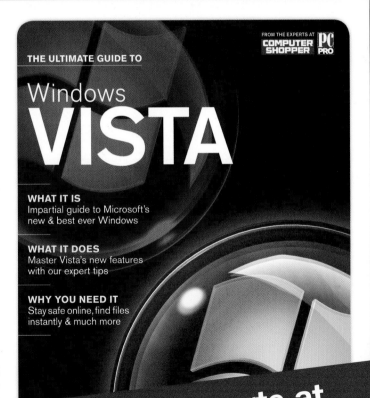

digital
Gallery

It's easy to get creative with digital technology. Plus it can hide a multitude of sins. Here are some of our favourite photo manipulations Facebook users have produced.

Gabrielle
I use this for my profile because I think it has an air of eeriness

Stuart
The electricity is real but the colour of my shirt has been changed digitally

Manda-Marie
It's a bit different from the usual pictures you see on Facebook – I changed the background so you can't see where it was taken!

Dennis
My friends and I were
messing around with my
webcam and this shot
made me laugh so much
I had to use it for my profile

Jenny
This is my favourite
because I thought
I was being panto
but people think I am
being porno. Oof!

Cheryl
This photo says
a lot about me,
It shows how
girly I am

Linda
This is Fi – the shot
is a nude which
was part of an
exhibition we did
called *Nude In
Support Of Aids
Community Care*

Lyckety
I had just done an
art project inspired
by *Sin City* and that
led to this piece

Next
Gallery
Everyone loves playing
dress-up, don't they?
Show off your fancy
pants on your profile
p60

Adding applications

Applications are one of the most fun aspects of Facebook, giving you the chance to interact with friends in new ways, play games online, or even organise your social life. Here's all you need to know about applications, and our pick of the best

Words **Alex Watson**

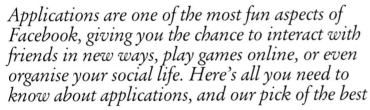

This way

Just as applications allow you to do more things on your computer, Facebook applications enable you to expand what you can do using the site and your profile. Despite the fact that they're a relatively new addition to Facebook, there were over 5,600 applications available at the time of writing, and the number is rising. The selection is incredibly varied, too, with applications ranging from the practical, such as calendars, to fun ones like multiplayer Scrabble and, of course, this being the internet, some rather bizarre ones invented by, you might suspect, some quite odd people.

Facebook applications need to be 'added' to your profile, but this is an easy process that's far simpler than installing software on your computer. There's no need to download any files, and no need to copy anything to your hard disk, or run any kind of complex installer. This is because all the available applications are stored on Facebook's own systems. All you need to do is pick the ones you want to use on your profile: in comparison to installing regular software, it's like ordering food

Installing Facebook apps is as simple as ordering something to eat from a restaurant menu

in a restaurant as opposed to cooking something yourself. Not only is it simple and quick, but because all the applications live, like your profile data, on Facebook's own servers, they're there for you to use whenever you log in to your account, whether you're in an internet cafe in Guatemala or sitting at your desk at work.

Generally speaking, Facebook applications are free. Some have been developed by large companies as tasters of their full products, others rely on advertising, and some solicit donations from fans. Just like computer applications, Facebook apps can be removed if you find they're less useful than you anticipated. ∎

Face facts

The top 10 applications are Video, My Questions, Graffiti, Top Friends, Superpoke!, X Me, Fortune Cookie, iLike, FreeGifts and Horoscopes – there are at least 4.5million users on the smallest of these.

▲ THERE are more than 5,600 applications available on Facebook, and that number is constantly rising

"How do I add an application?"

To add applications, start by clicking on 'Applications' at the top left of the screen

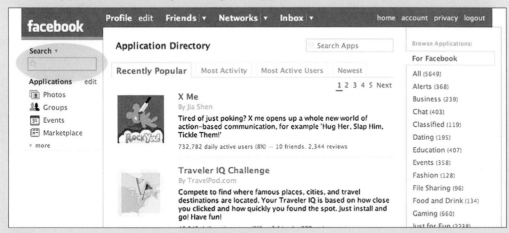

1 Click **'Browse More Applications'** to access Facebook's directory. All the possible choices are laid out here. There are a variety of ways to explore your choices on this screen. Have a look around, or if you want to find out about specific apps, you can read about them in this book (see p50 onwards). To find a specific application, type in the name in the **'Search'** box towards the top of the screen.

▲ ADDING new applications will keep your Facebook fresh and interesting

◀ A GOOD way to find applications you might like is to check the ones your friends have added

2 When you click on an application's name, you'll be taken to its summary screen. It's very similar to a group's home screen, as each app has a Wall, an area for discussions, and some statistics to view. It will also show you if any of your friends are using it, and provides links to the profiles of the developers. To install an app, click the big **'Add Application'** button at the top right of the screen.

Adding an application, continued...

3 Facebook will then ask you if you're sure that you want to do this, and present you with the only tricky part of the installation process. Applications need to be able to access your profile, so that they can display information there, and place a shortcut for you to use. They also like to be able to publish information about themselves to your News Feed – **'Alex added the XYZ App',** for instance. Some of these 'options' are truly optional – others are not. If you're worried about it, try deselecting the ones you're concerned about. Facebook will warn you if the options you have doubts over are strictly necessary in order for an application to function.

The **'Know Who I Am and access my information'** sounds the scariest, but it's also the one mandatory option. In part, forcing users to consent to this is Facebook covering themselves from any legal liability, but there's no getting away from the fact that agreeing to it exposes your profile to the application developers. However, if you've followed our advice so far and have thought about what you've put in your profile, then this shouldn't be a problem – all you're essentially doing is adding the developer as your friend. This option won't share anything more than what your friends can see, so your password, for instance, won't be exposed. As ever, the rule is to only put on Facebook what you're happy having out in public.

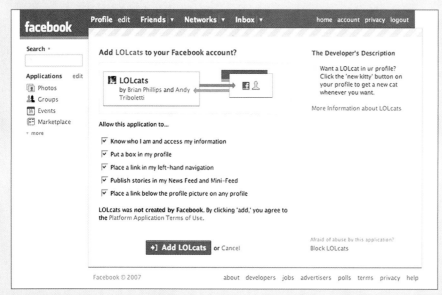

◄ CONSIDER your options when adding applications – for instance, you may not want it to contact your friends directly

4 Whether you should agree to 'Publish stories in my News Feed and Mini-Feed' is worth considering. This option essentially allows the app to publicise itself, and lets you shout about your own use of it. If it's a fun app like Ninjas vs Pirates that has a lot of updates, it's worth turning this option off, as it may irritate your friends to see hundreds of updates a day for it. And beware any app that asks if you want to send direct messages to your friends – unless your mates are all professional cold-callers it's unlikely they'll look kindly on you spamming them.

5 Once you've selected and deselected the options, click the big blue button and the app will be added to your profile. Facebook will then take you straight to the application. The way in which applications function differs from app to app, but some are relatively complex and contain multiple pages.

+] Add LOLcats or Cancel

Removing an app

■ Getting rid of a Facebook application is just as easy – if not easier – than installing one. On the main Facebook screen, simply click 'edit' next to the 'Applications' button at the top left.

▲ DON'T be scared to add apps – they can easily be dumped

▼ HOWEVER, if you add a lot, keep them well ordered

■ You'll then see a list of all your applications, along with clearly labelled links to edit their options or to remove them from your profile entirely. In the left-hand list of shortcuts to your apps you'll see a crosshair icon. When this is displayed, you can reorder the apps by dragging them. Put your most-used ones towards the top so that they're easier to get to.

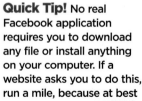

Quick Tip! No real Facebook application requires you to download any file or install anything on your computer. If a website asks you to do this, run a mile, because at best you're looking at a fake, and at worst at a virus-riddled, spyware-infected security nightmare.

Your first application

Now that you know what applications are all about, it's time to have some fun. And what better place to start than the world-conquering Scrabulous?

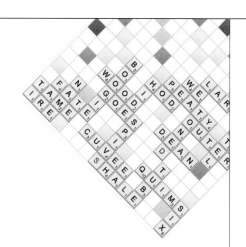

With thousands of different applications – all available at the low, low price of free – you might be wondering where exactly to start. The applications your friends are using are certainly worth exploring – as you'll see from our reviews of applications (p50 onwards), a great many of them only come to life when your friends are also using them.

 Matthew ▨▨▨▨▨▨ **is playing a video game.**
Eve Online, by CCP

 Matthew ▨▨▨▨ **added the** Video Games **application.**

■ Facebook will provide notifications when your friends add applications and also when they use their functions and, if you're interested in checking them out, simply click on the app where it shows up in your News Feed. However, to get you started, we're going to show you how to use Scrabulous, a Facebook application that allows you to play Scrabble against your friends. It's a great demonstration of the way Facebook applications can be fun, addictive and complex.

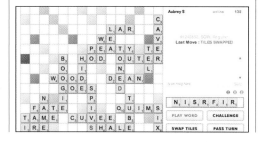

■ To get you started, first you need to install Scrabulous. Head to the Applications section, and type its name into the search bar. It will be top of the list. Once you've installed it, you'll see a screen listing your Facebook friends. Select up to three of them to play a game. You can add a personalised message to the challenge if you want. Use some big words or they'll think you're easy pickings!

■ Scrabulous is a well-mannered application – even if your friends don't have it installed, all they'll see is a polite notification under their Requests header. Once the request is sent, you can begin the game. You'll see it listed as active in the centre of the screen. Hit 'Play Your Turn' and the board will load.

Absolutely Scrabulous

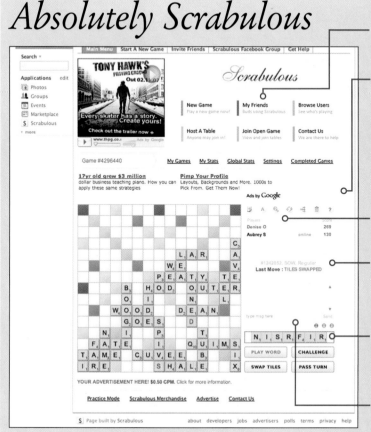

1. ACROSS THE top of the screen are a variety of colour-coded options, allowing you to go back to the list of games you're currently playing, settings, and, just as if you were a Premiership footballer, your stats.

2. ABOVE THE player list is a row of seven little grey icons. Hover your mouse over them and a window will pop up explaining what they do. All are tools that help with the game. The most useful are the first – it displays the list of eligible words – and the third, which lets you to look up letter combinations such as 'kwijibo' to see if they're actually valid words. Each grey button calls up a window that's superimposed over the board. To get back to the action, click the small red cross in the top-right-hand corner.

3. SCRABULOUS LISTS who's playing the game, and what their score is. Tip: You want your number to be bigger than theirs.

4. THIS IS THE last move – it's here that you can see if your opponent has given you an easy time or if they've reached deep into their lexicon to strike a deadly blow.

5. BENEATH THE chat window you can see the letters you've got to turn into linguistic gold dust. The three buttons just above the letters allow you to sort them A-Z, shuffle them, or clear them from the board.

6. THE MOST recent version of Scrabulous has added a chat window where you can type messages.

How to play Scrabulous

If you start the game you move first. As in the board game, your first word begins on the central tile, marked with a gold star. Drag your letters onto the board one at a time, then click PLAY WORD. The game will pause while it checks the word. If it's invalid, a red warning comes up. Keep trying, or just settle for a simple three-letter word. Now it's your opponent's turn. This can take a while, if your friends aren't Facebook junkies.

Luckily, Scrabulous lets you to have multiple games on the go at the same time. To start a new game, click either of the NEW GAME options at the top of the screen. Now you've got your first game under your belt, you can tinker with a few of the game settings before starting the second. Start typing the names of your friends in the box – up to four of you can play –

and beneath that you'll see drop-down menus allowing you to choose 'Dictionary' and 'Game Type'. There are two dictionaries – American, and 'rest of the world'. There are also two types of game. REGULAR is a fair fight to see who can get the most points; in CHALLENGE, you can try putting fake words down – it's up to your foes to challenge your embiggened expressions.

Once you're sick of pasting your friends, Scrabulous has an answer in its Open Table mode (just click the yellow button). Here, you can browse through games other users have set up where they need opponents.

Playing games on Facebook

Facebook isn't just wedding photos and poking your mates back and forth. Why not try being a zombie, a ninja, a pirate, or just taking on your friends at a good old-fashioned game of 'Pacman'

▲ PIRATES – can they defeat the ninjas?

The existence of 'games' on Facebook implies that the core of Facebook is somehow work, which, as a proposition, would probably find the same amount of support as the average tax rise. Still, there are plenty of apps you can add to your account that are explicitly about fun. That doesn't, however, mean that they are actually fun. Plenty are basically spam-machines dressed up as games, but there are some gems out there.

Zombies

■ The most popular game on Facebook is 'Zombies', whose name gives away the core focus of the app. You start off as an 'Ensign Zombie Newbie' – for some reason these zombies like their naval nomenclature – and have to 'fight' other zombies to progress up the ranks. It's pretty tame stuff by game standards, as the fight only involves a mouse click, and spamming your friends with invites is a key part of success.

Pirates Vs Ninjas

■ 'Pirates Vs Ninjas' has an awesome name, based on a popular internet meme, or fad, which posits the following zen-like riddle: Who would win in a fight – pirates or ninjas? It also has due cause for its nautical terminology, but sadly it's essentially the same game as 'Zombies', requiring you to pressgang your friends into service in order to earn yourself points.

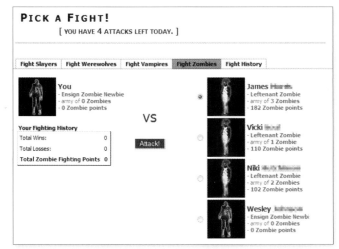

PICK A FIGHT!

[YOU HAVE 4 ATTACKS LEFT TODAY.]

Fight Slayers | Fight Werewolves | Fight Vampires | Fight Zombies | Fight History

You
- Ensign Zombie Newbie
- army of 0 Zombies
- 0 Zombie points

Your Fighting History
Total Wins: 0
Total Losses: 0
Total Zombie Fighting Points 0

VS

Attack!

James ▉▉▉▉
- Leftenant Zombie
- army of 3 Zombies
- 182 Zombie points

Vicki ▉▉▉
- Leftenant Zombie
- army of 1 Zombie
- 110 Zombie points

Niki ▉▉ ▉▉▉▉▉
- Leftenant Zombie
- army of 2 Zombies
- 102 Zombie points

Wesley ▉▉▉ ▉▉▉▉▉
- Ensign Zombie Newbi
- army of 0 Zombies
- 0 Zombie points

Pirates

■ The more plainly named 'Pirates' brings the core activities of being a pirate to life with a little bit more swagger than 'Pirates Vs Ninjas', especially as it doesn't make you feel like you're working for a direct-mail marketing company. When you first add the app, you need to choose what type of pirate you want to be, and you can then navigate around the world, searching for treasure, battles, and Keira Knightley, by clicking in the manner of an old-school 80s adventure game. There's a decent number of activities to take part in – you can search islands for treasure, go gambling in port and upgrade your ship, too.

▶ GET YOUR very own shiny lightsaber when you sign up to 'Jedi Vs Sith'

▼ GAMBLING and hunting for buried treasure are par for the course in 'Pirates'

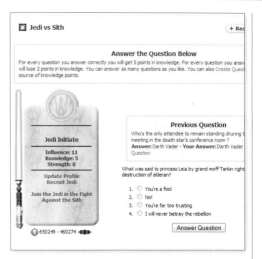

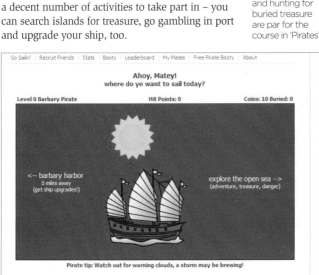

Jedi Vs Sith

■ For a website, Facebook is resolutely non-geeky. That doesn't mean there isn't room for *Star Wars*, though. 'Jedi Vs Sith' doesn't quite get to the core of the *Star Wars* experience – there's no John Williams music, for instance – but equally, it's not a total muppet-laden travesty in the mould of *Episode 1*. Like some other games, it does encourage you to sign up friends in exchange for points, but you can also boost your character by answering *Star Wars* trivia questions – which character has the last line in the ending of *A New Hope*, etc – and there's even a hint the app may one day encompass the vastness of the *Star Wars* universe. Still, it's most fun when your friends are using it and you can battle each other. Plus, what other app gives you your own lightsaber?

Pacman

■ 'Pacman' is an absolute gem – it's a perfectly executed copy of the original game, complete with bleepy-bloopy sound effects, power pills and ever-escalating levels of difficulty. The game's best feature is that it neatly integrates the high scores of friends who also have it installed, displaying them at the end of your game so that you're forever chasing their targets – or setting one for them to chase.

Warbook

■ 'Warbook' is one of the most complex and fun original games for Facebook. In it, you manage a kingdom and must defend against other players, while at the same time trying to increase your territory. It's a very numerical game to look at, but the developers have done their best to smarten it up and the interface is simple and easy to grasp. Not only that, but in a manner that is not the case with many Facebook applications, the developers have taken the time to write a comprehensive help file (http://optimus.freewebz.com/help), which will get you quickly up to speed. Your key choices are whether you spend your time and resources building your army, expanding your empire, or going out conquering. As with all successful empires, the key is actually to keep the books balanced while you rampage around the world – expand too quickly and you'll go broke as well as be targeted by enemies.

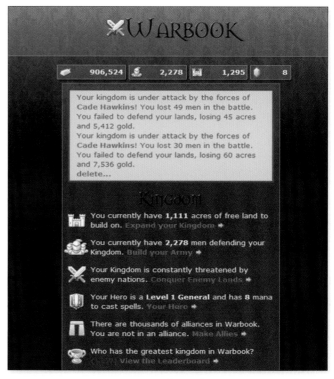

'Pacman' is a perfectly executed copy of the original videogame, complete with all the bleeps

▲ WARBOOK lets you virtually devastate your best friends
◀ COMPETE with friends for top score on 'Pacman'

Doing more with your wall

Back in the 80s, 'the Wall' would either mean prog rock or the big concrete dividing line that cut Berlin unhappily in two. Facebook's walls are – fortunately – neither as ponderous nor as divisive, being far closer to public noticeboards than anything built of bricks. By default, your contacts can only leave text messages on your wall, but several of Facebook's most popular applications allow you to expand the features of your wall – or rather, replace it entirely with a wall that people can draw on, or pin pictures and video to. Here are a couple of them:

Quick tip! As with posts on the default Facebook wall, posts to added walls are publicly displayed in your profile, so you need to trust your friends won't do anything too embarrassing with these apps. Failing that, just have Facebook open all day long and be ready to delete.

Super Wall & Fun Wall

Jo Clements wrote
at 12:52pm on November 03

Lionel Richtea

Hello....................
is it tea you're lookin' for...

Shine

Glitter

Color Hearts

Thought

Sparkles

Super Wall
● Super Wall is the marginally more popular of the two biggest wall apps. Somewhat annoyingly, your friends will also need to add the app if they want to use yours. Super Wall allows people to add free-form drawings to the wall, along with pictures and video. The 'Draw Graffiti' option is easily its best feature; there's a colour mixer and basic brush controls – sure, it's not very advanced, but there are enough options to let you draw a wonky cartoon owl, and allow some guy called Ryan Kirkman to paint a portrait of Van Gogh.

FunWall
● FunWall is a little annoying to install, because it bugs you to send invites to all your contacts, but once it's actually on your profile it's slightly more flexible than Super Wall, because people don't need it installed themselves to post on yours. Its features are similar – you can post photos, videos and 'Make a Sketch', which is all but identical to the 'Graffiti' portion of Super Wall. The one feature FunWall has that its rival lacks is 'Funpix'. This allows you to load images – by default, it's those tagged with your name – then add lots of crazy effects to them.

Most popular applications

Top Friends
● Three million Facebook users have this app installed, despite the fact it's little more than a giant popularity contest and spam machine.

Video
● Facebook's own video app makes it easy to share moving pictures of your friends.

SuperPoke!
● SuperPoke! takes Facebook's built in 'poke' feature to *Spinal Tap* levels of excess, allowing you to virtually

prod, slap, hug and hurl sheep at your Facebook friends.

My Questions
● "Could Aaron's anger cause him to explode?" Ask any or all of your friends a question. They answer, then it's their turn.

Compare People
● Rank your friends in categories – most popular, most entertaining, best-looking. Potential for fall-out is huge.

Further applications

Fun with your pets, loving your enemies, and an amazing app that learns what kind of music you like, then works out what else you'd enjoy, and tells you about it…

Where I've Been

● **What is it?** A map that allows you to show your friends where you've travelled

'Where I've Been' is not an app that radiates *je ne sais quoi* – its straightforward name gives away exactly what it does. It places a map of the globe on your profile; click on the countries you've visited and your friends can then see where you've been. Clicking more than once allows you to indicate if you've lived in a certain place, or if you simply want to visit it. When friends add the application, you can easily see their maps, and while there's a certain showiness to listing all the places you've been to, chatting about travel is a great way to get to know people. You might find people have been to places you're interested in, and the addition of the 'Travel Chat' option to the app – where you can talk to other users – shows the developers have got some interesting plans for the future.

● Rating: ★★★☆☆

It's simple and showy, but still cool (and not remotely imperialistic, oh no) to see how much of the world you've conquered.

My Flickr

● **What is it?** A classy photo showcase
● **Requirements** Free Flickr account

Yahoo's Flickr (Flickr.com) is a photo website with a range of excellent features for storing your own images and exploring those of others. 'My Flickr' is a way of getting your Flickr images onto your Facebook profile. While Facebook's own photo app is a decent way to share pictures of your mates, 'My Flickr' is more of an artistic showcase, with a range of controls allowing you to make the best of your images. Flickr was one of the first websites to support tagging of images, and the My Flickr app can be set to only show images with a certain tag. So if you want to only put up your images of London, or taken with a certain lens, that's easy (provided, of course, you've been organised when uploading photos to Flickr), and you can also limit images based on date criteria. The app allows you to stipulate how many images to put on your profile. And you can add a border, too – oooooh!

● Rating: ★★★★☆

It can be a little fiddly, but My Flickr has a ton of options and will do justice to your best pictures.

Most pointless applications

○ **Dramatic Whitespace**
Minimalists rejoice! Or at least smile in a cool, restrained manner. If you're fed up with cluttered profiles and want to add some white space to Facebook, 'Dramatic Whitespace' is the answer.

○ **Pointless Game**
"A really simple game where you fight others for no real reason other than to be the most powerful," it boasts.

○ **Bob Dylan**
The Dylan app takes the iconic video to 'Subterranean Homesick Blues', strips out all the words (since when were Dylan's words important?) and allows you to add in your own message instead. Links to his anaemic new 'Best Of' are also included.

○ **Oktoberfest Party**
Virtual drinking? We don't think so.

Catbook

● **What is it?** It's like Facebook, but for cats
● **Requirements** A cat

Some humans go ga-ga over cats and technology – while cats, of course, seem to care very little for either. The fact cats are both disdainful and lacking in opposable thumbs means you, their human butler, will need to work 'Catbook' for your cat. The app is essentially a total clone of Facebook, only for your moggy: you can upload pictures, list your cat's favourite treats and add other felines as friends. Admirers can leave fawning messages on your puss's wall, and instead of poking, there's stroking. While it might not seem like the best idea for an app in the world, it's actually quite useful to be able to separate out your cat's life from your own when it comes to Facebook, as you can be as silly as you like with one, and serious with the other. Your choice of which is which, of course, depending on how much you dote on your pet.
● **Rating:** ★ ★ ★ ★ ☆
It's got more features than Enemybook, and cat fans will like being able to fully document their pet's life. Yes, there's a canine version – Dogbook.

SuperPoke!

● **What is it?** Poking is for amateurs. Real Facebookers throw sheep

'SuperPoke!' is one of Facebook's most popular applications, and like 'Free Gifts', it takes one of the site's own features – the poke – and amps it up to 11. While Facebook only allows you to poke people, with SuperPoke! you can hug, high-five or even chuck a sheep at people. Makes you glad Facebook isn't real, right? Well, that's just for starters. In classic videogame style, the more you play, the more options you unlock, with options ranging from 'drunk dialing' to 'using the force' available at higher levels. Cynics may say it's basically a spam application – if you SuperPoke! anyone without the application, they get a message asking them to install it, which may go some way to explaining why it has a monstrous 1.4million users – but for the most part it's a fun, if pointless piece of Facebook nerdery.
● **Rating:** ★ ★ ★ ☆ ☆
Throwing sheep at your friends might be a bit of fun, but it's not the most useful application in the world.

Enemybook

● **What is it?** A way to keep track of your bitterest enemies
● **Requirements** A nemesis

Facebook allows you to keep your friends close, so it's only natural that it's also pretty handy for keeping your enemies even closer. Once you've added 'Enemybook', the app calls up your contact list and snidely asks which "so-called" friend you want to add as an enemy. It then cleverly inverts Facebook's 'add friend' procedure, asking you to explain why you're their enemy – there's even a 'we became enemies randomly' option to use, particularly useful if you're Nicolas Cage and you're trying to explain the plot of one of your recent movies. However, once you've added someone as your enemy, there's not really much you can do, other than 'flip' them off. There's also a global chart of enemies to peruse. Unsurprisingly, Dubya is number one.
● Rating: ★★☆☆☆
It's a nice idea but it's more of a shallow dalliance than a life-long feud.

Friendwheel

● **What is it?** A cool way of visualising the connections between your friends

One of the most pleasant surprises you can have using Facebook is finding out how friends are linked – trace the connections through friends and friends and Facebook can make it seem like a very small world indeed. 'Friendwheel' is a tool for visualising the way your friends are connected. Download the app, and you'll see a variety of options. Ignore these the first time you use it, as you'll only see what they do once you've got an idea of how the app works. Click 'Generate' at the bottom and you'll soon see a colourful wheel with your name in the centre. Each spoke is the name of a friend. Lines are drawn between friends who are friends of each other, and they're all sorted into colour-coded groups. The 'Flash Wheel' mode makes it interactive, allowing you to move friends around and zoom in and out.
● Rating: ★★★★☆
Computerising your life with sites like Facebook might seem dry at first, but 'Friendwheel' is an excellent example of the way data can be interpreted in an artistic way.

Taking your status updates further

Want to supercharge your status update? Read on to see how you can post what you're up to by sending a humble text message, and get sent streams of interesting websites

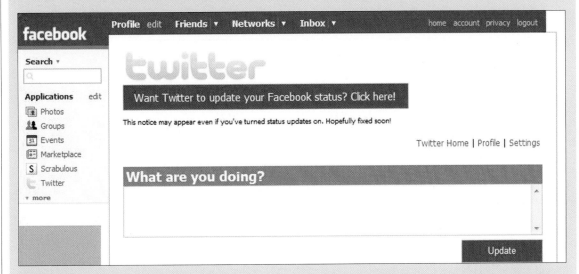

Twitter

● **What Is It?** A flexible micro-blogging system

Twitter asks people to answer the question 'What are you doing?' in no more than 140 characters – making responses similar in length to a text message. You can follow friends' updates, as well as those from a massive range of companies and organisations, and, as the system is open and flexible, there's a huge range of Twitter programmes which allow you to update the service from your PC and mobile phone.

The Facebook application enables you to follow Twitter contacts inside Facebook, and to post updates to Twitter. The most recent version also lets you make your Twitter updates your Facebook 'status updates'.

Once you've installed the application, it will prompt you to log in to your Twitter account, and if you don't have one, there's a link to the sign-up page. If you do need to sign up for an account, once you've completed the form, you won't be automatically taken back to

Facebook, so head back there to finish setting up the Facebook application. Once you've logged in, the final step is to click the big button which says 'Want Twitter to update your Facebook status?' to tie the two together.

It's now time to start firing updates to Twitter about how you're doing. The beauty is you don't need to be on Facebook to do this. If you're on a Mac, Twitterific (Iconfactory.com/software/twitterrific) is a beautiful piece of software that lives discreetly in the menu bar at the top of the screen. On Windows, Twitteroo (Rareedge.com/twitteroo/) is well worth a look. You can also update your status from your mobile: simply send a text message to +44 (0)7624 801 423.

Some organisations are also using Twitter, and adding them as friends can bring interesting and funny news into your Facebook life. There's the BBC (Twitter.com/bbcnews) and *The New York Times* (Twitter.com/nytimes), a competition which sends out first lines of novels for you to guess (Twitter.com/twitterlituk) and even Darth Vader is on it (Twitter.com/darthvader).

YouTube Box
● **What is it?** Brings the 'book and the 'Tube closer together

YouTube and Facebook have colonised a lot of people's spare (and not so spare) time online, their bandwidth, attention, and even the colours red and blue for their respective logos. 'YouTube Box' is a nifty Facebook application that allows you to integrate your favourite videos from all those hours of YouTube research with your Facebook profile. It's a fairly sophisticated app, allowing you to add multiple videos and re-order them before you actually make them public on your profile. Once this is done, your friends can watch them there and then without ever having to ever leave Facebook. You can also use YouTube Box to post links from other video sites (provided they provide code for embedding), along with photos and mp3s.
● **Rating:** ★★★★☆
Simple and well-thought-out, YouTube Box is a great little application that builds on the video-sharing of Facebook's own 'Posted Items' app.

Last.fm
● **What is it?** Display recently played music, find new stuff to listen to
● **Requirements** Free Last.fm account

Last.fm lets you track music you listen to on your computer. By monitoring which songs you listen to, and comparing it to the data from thousands of other people, the system comes up with recommendations, and using the Facebook app, you can listen to these. If you click on the Last.fm link in your list of applications on the left of the screen, you'll see a list of 10 artists similar to your current taste. If you load your profile, and scroll down to the Last.fm box, you'll see there are two tabs to the app: 'Radio' and 'Recently Played'. Click the big 'play' button on the Radio tab and the system will start playing tracks it hopes you'll like. You can skip ahead if the song is as appealing as an *X Factor* reject, but if it's your taste click 'Play me music like this'. It won't be long before you'll be burning mix CDs full of obscure Canadian indie music for your friends.
● **Rating:** ★★★★★
The ability to explore new music makes Last.fm a killer app.

Quick tip! If you'd prefer to focus on simply displaying the songs you've been listening to recently, the 'What I'm Listening To' app is a less-cluttered alternative to Last.fm's official application, although it still requires you to use a Last.fm account.

Blogging and link-sharing on Facebook

Facebook's core features are ideal for communicating on a one-to-one basis, but it can also be used for addressing a group (or all) of your friends and sharing links among the group. If you're already using a blog for this kind of writing, you can integrate that into Facebook, too.

Posted Items & Notes

● **What is it?** These two default apps enable you to use your profile to blog and share your thoughts and interesting finds

'Posted Items' and 'Notes' have both been developed by Facebook and are included by default – however, they're usually hidden so you need to click 'More' at the bottom of your left-hand list of apps to reveal them.

'Posted Items' is ideal for sharing links on a one-off basis – if you've just launched a website, or uploaded a video to YouTube, or found a hilarious cat picture your friends should all see, this is the app for you. When you click on 'Posted Items', most of the screen will be taken up by the items your friends have shared. Just as with many blogs, you can add a comment to any of the items.

To share your own finds, start by typing, or pasting the link into the box at the top right. Facebook will then scan it and look for a picture in the page to use to illustrate the link. If it finds more than one, you can scroll through the pictures, and add some text to describe what oddities you're promoting. Two tabs at the top allow you to choose between sending the link directly to just a few friends, or posting it for everyone to see on your news feed.

If you want to share more text, then 'Notes' is the app for you. As with 'Posted Items', by default it shows you what your friends have been up to. At the top of the screen you can filter the feed by contact, so if there's someone you really want to hear from, it's easy to find their items. There's even the possibility of formatting text using HTML code, and Facebook has a handy cheat sheet here: Facebook.com/ notes_cheatsheet.php.

◀ 'POSTED ITEMS' is ideal for sharing links with friends on a one-off basis

◀ 'NOTES' performs a similar function, and is useful if you want to share more text

Gallery

fancy dress

On Facebook you have minimum space to make maximum impact. Playing dress-up makes for a more colourful and interesting profile picture.

David
One lunch hour we found a pile of expensive clothes in a photo studio and came up with this, my superhero alter-ego. I call him 'The Golden Retriever'

Danielle
This is me and my mates at our work Christmas do as drunk *Batman* characters. Don't know who the bloke is, though!

Rhiannon
My girlfriend and I in her backyard, getting ready for a night out

Dave
I like to dress as a monkey for parties. But sometimes it all gets too much for me...

Stuart
This look may not appear
that great at first glance,
but believe me, it sure as hell
gets the ladies. Cheers!

Mitch
This is me at Shambala
Festival 2007. I decided
to be a *Clockwork Orange*
droog for the day

Janine
This is me as fat drunk
Elvis. Every February
I dress up like this to DJ.
I look strangely like my
mother in this picture

Nadia
A friend of mine had an
80s-themed birthday party.
I snagged the purple coat for £4

Brody
This is last Halloween's
outfit. I was a zombie

Andy
It was taken
as a homage to
a Michael Caine
photo used to
promote *Get Carter*

Next Gallery
The zoo and you!
Monkeys, birds, a blind
giraffe... animal pictures
make us laugh
p70

Face facts

The name Facebook was derived from the paper 'facebooks' given to staff and students at American universities on arrival.

Famous Facers

Why on earth would celebrities go on Facebook? Because actually, celebrities are a bit like people. Some of them want to be adored, others just want to show they're Just Like You And Me. Here are some of the best (genuine) Famous Facers out there

Words **Chris Bourn**

This way

or celebrities, Facebook is Hell.com. Imagine it – from the moment you signed up it'd be like psychological torture. First you'd set up your profile, only to realise there are already multiple versions of you roaming around, hoodwinking your more gullible friends and recent girlfriends into embarrassing chit-chat. (There are, for example, at least 24 John Malkoviches on the loose on Facebook, not all of them spelt correctly.)

Then within a couple of days the stalkers and haters would arrive at your wall like wasps at a barbecue, showering it in hot, fizzy kisses and bile respectively. Meanwhile, everything from the fish in your aquarium to the party you've not been invited to are up there, tasty morsels for any crumb-catching hack to snatch away and dish up as a full English breakfast in tomorrow's tabloids.

But amid the herd of fakers and tribute sites, proper, real-life, talk-to-my-agent celebrities have been stampeding onto Facebook along with the rest of us. So why would these people, who've dedicated their lives to hauling themselves above the crowd and onto the stage, want to turn around and hurl themselves back into the moshpit?

Clearly, a few celebs are on there just to further their careers. Everywhere-celebrities like Jimmy Carr and Russell Brand are as inescapable on Facebook as they are on telly. Their PR-managed profiles turn up in every high-profile friend list you come across – but it's all just flyering for upcoming tour dates and has nothing to do with getting within sniffing distance of their fans.

Less-driven comics, like Nick Frost and David Baddiel, no doubt signed up because their mates did. They're on there primarily to have a lark.

For much bigger names, Facebook offers the chance to be anonymous again.

Then there are Facebook's men and women of the people – the handful of fearless celebs with an open-door policy, who actually seem to enjoy hanging out with their public online. Why? Because celebrities, more than any other type of child, crave attention – and for every insult-spitting loon, a solid, likeable B-lister can pull at least 50 admirers who'll

Why do celebs, who've spent their lives scrabbling onto the stage, hurl themselves back into the moshpit?

gush about how funny, talented or sexy they were on *100 Most Ordinary Soapstar Haircuts* last night.

But somewhere in a deep recess of their charity-bothering hearts lies stars' real motivation for braving Facebook's prole onslaught. It's the same reason none of us can leave the thing alone: numbers, baby. A Facebook friends list is the simplest, most precise measure of a person's popularity yet devised. And popularity equals celebrity. Does Jonathan Ross – famously the talent sitting on the hugest salary at the BBC by a big country pile – really care how many fewer Facebook friends he has than his mate Stephen Fry? Yes, he pwobably does… ∎

Early adopters

○ **Jo Whiley (pictured), Radio 1 DJ:**
"It's good to know there are freaks out there like me who hate egg whites and think that raisins taste like dead flies… For me, it's all about the groups."

○ **Krishnan Guru-Murthy, Channel 4 news presenter:**
"I opened it because everyone else was using it. I never 'got' MySpace."

○ **Charlie Brooker, TV critic:**
Signed up in May because all his friends were doing it, saying, "Even misanthropes hate feeling left out."

○ **Sir Menzies Campbell, MP, Former Lib Dem leader:**
Keen silver surfer Ming, 67, was one of the first Westminster names to use Facebook as a political tool. By June this year he had more than 1,700 friends and 200 photos up.

○ **Sir Patrick Moore, 84, Astronomer, xylophone player:**
"I was told about Facebook by some young camera crew I was working with, and I was intrigued about how people are able to communicate these days."

Stephen Fry

Friend-swamped cuddly couch-face

When it comes to the sacred institution of British manners, Stephen Fry always has the last word. That's why his experience, as one of the first big celebs to throw open his profile to the public, illustrates perfectly how Facebook can be a terrifying minefield for the famous.

It might surprise you to know Stephen is a huge gadgets nerd. His wit-laden musings on the latest mobile phones, iPods and palm-pilots is a regular theme of his blog at Stephenfry.com, and he says he is "constitutionally unable to coexist with new technology without wishing to penetrate its mysteries".

So in July 2007, as Facebook reached its tipping point, he hurled himself into it like a schoolgirl into a pillowfight, making it policy to accept to his friend list anyone who asked nicely. But within a week he was receiving 150 friend requests a day and it all got too much. Smothered by love, but far too fluffy a human being to turn his back on a well-wisher, he beat an honourable retreat, and set up a group called 'Stephen Fry's Facebook Proxy Group' as a holding pen for his exploding army of buddies.

By November, the group had 9,000 members and it's still growing at a blistering rate. It makes his assurance that he'll "look in as often as I can and answer questions if I am able" appear a bit feeble – but you sympathise when he says: "Thanks for being here, it's stopped me having to run from Facebook altogether."

Jonathan Ross

Foppy high-tax-bracket mispronouncer

He's got a chatshow 4.3million people watch every Friday, a Saturday slot on Radio 2 that's one of the most popular on the air, his own production company (Hotsauce) and three kids and a wife he's devoted to. So how does Britain's floppiest fringe find time to mess about on an open Facebook profile boasting 2,869 friends? And even more baffling, how does he manage to be one of the most active – and interactive – celeb Facebook users online? Only God and Jonathan Ross know. It's quite possible they're the same person.

His success at social networking is partly to do with the fact he's a man with a superhuman capacity for talk. Among his Facebook friends (most of whom are fans) he has a reputation for responding in person and quickly. And he has a track record for mucking in like a proper, down-to-earth person. He recently responded personally to a blog criticising his production company for asking YouTube to take down video clips. A series of frank emails later, and he'd switched his company's policy, to allow clips to stay on YouTube.

Jonathan swerves many of the problems of being a celeb Facebooker by not having a wall. Instead, he does all his messaging one-on-one, The proof? When one girl asked him to write on her wall so she'd win an office bet, he swiftly obliged – the only real response on a wall full of celebrity fakers – saying: "Hi Vicky. With the power invested in me, what with an OBE an all, I hereby endorse your campaign to get lots of famous names on your wall. Good Luck. Jonathan."

Goldie

*Treasure-toothed ex-*EastEnders *junglist*

The man who helped make drum'n'bass popular in the 90s has had his finger in many pies over the years – soap-acting pie, breakdancing pie, international-grill-trader pie, Björk pie... But on his Facebook page it's his achievements as a graffiti artist in Wolverhampton he gives top billing, even above his music career. We also find out where he got his name from – not his trademark gold teeth, but the blond dreadlocks he used to have in the 80s.

- **Friends:** 581 and counting.
- **Famous friends:** Darren Emerson, DJ Fabio.
- **Best group membership:** 'I Hope Ricky Hatton Gives Floyd Mayweather A Fucking Good Hiding'.
- **Best wall post:** A recipe for pan-fried salmon cakes from a female fan in China.

Gok Wan

Stylish telly camper-upper

Gok, bless him, is an utter Facebook whore. But a charming one. His profile page is as camp and as bitchy as the undressing dressings-down he dishes out on Channel 4's *How To Look Good Naked*. Among his interests he lists being a "shopaholic and manaholic", and he is, in his own words, "vain, arrogant, but a really nice guy at heart!"

- **Friends:** 370 and counting.
- **Famous friends:** Jodie Harsh.
- **Best wall post:** This, from Cindy, who Gok gave a makeover to: "Hi Gok, Thank you from the bottom of my heart, you've changed the direction of my life to a very confident and truly happy one. PS: On the way home in the minibus, Little Princess Miah asked me and her dad if she could live with you during the weekdays and come home for weekends." Ahhh...

Edgar Wright

Gag-writing Tassie Devil

The filmmaking furball behind *Spaced, Shaun Of The Dead* and *Hot Fuzz* is a whirlwind – a 1,000mph phenomenon of scattergun ideas and movie-obsessed gabble. And he applies the same hyperspace-velocity nerdery to his Facebook. It's actually pretty riveting: an hour-by-hour captain's log of the films he's watching, the awards he's winning and his life touring the world to promote *Hot Fuzz* – all with hundreds of funny pictures and captions. If you've ever wondered what directors do all day when they're not shouting 'Cut!', it's all here. Fascinating.

- **Edgar's life in status updates (highlights):**
  27 Sep 2007: "Edgar is on his fourth espresso and has caffeine whiplash."
  29 Sep 2007: "Edgar is stunned to report we won the damn award. Check out ITV1 tonight. See if they cut my *Blue Peter* cat joke."
  7 Oct 2007: "Edgar is sorry he only got to see half of *Creepshow* before doing a bunch of press. But he watched *Hot Fuzz* with a 1,000-strong crowd. Awesome."

The Mitchell Brothers

Geezery Cockney rhyming slangers

Mike Skinner's East End hip-hop mates the Mitchell Brothers (technically cousins) share a single profile. This puts them eternally on the wrong side of the universal 'is' update cue on the Facebook status line – for instance: "The Mitchell Brothers is looking forward to the Calvin Harris tour..." Grammatically incorrect, but they sort of get away with it because it's a bit street.

- **Friends:** 437 and counting.
- **Famous friends:** Carl Barat.
- **Best wall post:** "Stop putting baby lotion on ur head before performances! It could be dangerous!"

Natasha Bedingfield

Snakey baby-wanting pop streak

Tash's record company has done a good job of getting her profile – armed with a picture of her album cover – everywhere you look on Facebook. Nevertheless, she seems to knock around on it from time to time, and the page is loaded with fan-pleasing goodies – previews of her videos, candid tour photos, songs and regular chirpy blog posts from the lady herself. The overall message she's putting out seems to be: Talk to me – I'm not as weird as my brother.

- **Friends:** 4,895.
- **Famous friends:** David Gest.
- **Most unexpected group membership:** VW Club South Africa – discussion group for people trying to get hold of Volkswagen cars and parts in South Africa.
- **Most annoyed wall message:** From a Kent University student: "I can't say that I am complaining but I think my Facebook status should be, 'Dave is confused as to why Natasha wants to be mates with him...' Any thoughts???"

NATASHA is a big fan of sourcing VW car parts in South Africa, it would seem

Dead heads

Facebook has even made it to the afterlife. Here are seven sparkling celebrities who are keeping out of trouble by Facebooking from beyond the grave:

 Oliver Reed: Profile dedicated to sending virtual booze to the greatest liver in history.

 Mike Reid: Wall with the largest number of messages containing the word 'Ricky' on Facebook.

 Tony Hancock: "... is smoking weed in Heaven," apparently, where he's mates with Kurt Cobain.

 Euripides: The most popular Ancient Greek tragedian on Facebook.

 Beethoven: The composer, not the dog. Facebook friends with Mr JS Bach.

 Marlon Brando (in character as Don Vito Andolini-Corleone): Friend request you simply can't refuse.

 Jesus H Christ: Member of the network 'Israel'. Presumably here because he couldn't get a *Second Life* account.

67

Darren Emerson
Shouting Ibiza-botherer

Former Underworld mixmaster and current fiancé of ex-*X Factor* presenter Kate Thornton, Darren is 'avin' it large on Facebook at the moment. He's doing the zombies and vampires thing (Vampire Warrior, 88 points); he's sorted for stripper names (Tony Nightknocker), human pets, drinks, X-Mes, Superpokes and wall graffiti; and among his top TV shows he's dropping, er, *Time Team* and *Spring Watch*. As befits his superstar-DJ lifestyle he's a high-energy, heavy-throttle, crowd-pleasing, qwerty-banging Facebook monster! Go on, Dazza!

- **Friends:** 1,118 and counting.
- **Famous friends:** Jade Jagger, Jamie Cullum, Goldie, Holly Willoughby, Lisa Moorish, Erol Alkan (fellow DJ), Arthur Baker (New York superproducer).
- **Sole iLike song:** 'To Cut A Long Story Short' by Spandau Ballet.

Matt Goss
Growly 80s-pop jean-tearer

The singing half of blond denim-shredding 80s sensation Bros is using Facebook as a platform to relaunch his music career. With Take That's and Westlife's comebacks well underway, he may have missed the slot for 80s-boyband reunions. But that hasn't stopped his people from setting up an 'OFFICIAL' Facebook page on Matt's behalf, and issuing a coldly delivered threat that "Matt is in the studio working on new music."

- **Friends:** 710 and counting.
- **Friends' average age:** 32.
- **Best wall post:** "Oh God, the shame – I am so sorry for sending you a disgustingly inappropriate question – I am dying of shame if it helps. If there is a God, you won't have opened it. PLEASE don't let this be the real Matt Goss…" (Question not quoted.)

Jakki Degg
Party-mad Page 3 boob show-er

Partly for her vivaciousness but mostly for her getting-her-boobs-out-ness, Jakki is one of Page 3's most popular alumni ever. Which is why many men struggle to believe it's really her being all flirty and perky and emailable on Facebook. Via her site, you can 'vibrate her hamster', or even challenge her to a hand of poker. She's supposed to be a pure, unobtainable sex fantasy, dammit. But, in her own words: "I joined Facebook because my MySpace has become more for people that appreciate my work… I am not going to deny people friendship, but I really don't appreciate people I don't know calling me a fake. If you don't think this is me that's fine, but I'm just a normal person that has friends like everyone else." OK, OK, we believe you. Sheesh.

- **Friends:** 4,994 (maxed out).
- **Famous friends:** Lots and lots of glamour models.
- **Friends demographic:** Roughly 80% male, in their early 20s, trying to look cool holding pints
- **Scariest friend:** Cupid Valentino – a butterfly-collector's profile "set up with the aim of attracting the best-looking women on the entire Facebook social network" (so far he has 44).
- **Most-given gift:** A pair of pink frilly knickers, often with a message, eg: "U left these on the floor of my room the other night."

Product placebook

Uh-oh. Here come the Facebook publicity-mongers – and here's how they're working it

Russell Brand Is...

"... unable to add more friends as he's reached the Facebook 5,000 limit!!" (21 Oct 2007)
And whose fault is that, Russell? Your busy PR beavers, that's whose.
Russell has been recruiting: "People to make jingles for his show." (20 Oct 2007)
Russell has been selling: "Two new dates for the Roundhouse show 14 & 15 Dec. Tickets are onsale now Ticketzone.co.uk." (19 Oct 2007)
Russell has been fishing for: "Suggestions on who his co-host could be this week? Email Russell.brand@bbc.co.uk with your suggestions, along with anything else we might find amusing." (16 Oct 2007)
Strategy: Dresden.

Dom Joly Is...

"... in the Facebook doghouse." The shouty pranker's wall recently suffered a glut of angry comments after hundreds of Facebookers mysteriously received an invite to a Dom Joly-hosted 'event' that turned out to be nothing more than the release date of his book, *Letters To My Golf Club*. Bit of a mishit there, Dom... fore!
Strategy: Slapstick.

Brian Dowling Is...

"... doesn't maintain his own profile, but he does get all fanmail and reads the comments." Thanks for being upfront, Bri. Medal on its way.
Brian was, lest we forget: "The first gay winner of *BB* in the world, and received a still-unbeaten 4.23million votes. Since then has been voted the UK's favourite *BB* housemate of all time."
Brian recently: "Spent two weeks in ITV1's *Hell's Kitchen*, becoming an accomplished pastry chef... He came a respectable third."
Strategy: Blind optimism.

Jimmy Carr Is...

"...in Portsmouth on Friday, Brighton on Saturday and Sunday for the comedy festival." (21 Oct 2007)
Jimmy's four favourite movies are: *Confetti, I Want Candy, Alien Autopsy* and *Stormbreaker* (all starring Jimmy Carr).
Jimmy's favourite book is: *The Naked Jape*, by Jimmy Carr and Lucy Greeves.
Jimmy Carr's six favourite quotes of all time are: All Jimmy Carr jokes. Such as: "I was asked to judge Mr Gay UK. I said no problem at all: he's against nature and God, and he's going to hell."
Strategy: Stalinism.

Booked 2007

Celebs who've fallen foul of Facebook's be-on-your-best-behaviour bylaws

Princess Eugenie York

● In July, Fergie and Prince Andrew's 17-year-old daughter – sixth in line to the throne – joined a Facebook group called 'Tassilo is a Spearchucker'. The princess's apparent endorsement of casual racism sparked a storm among media and equality groups. For the historical record, Tassilo is white – and a descendent of the 19th-century German chancellor Otto von Bismarck. You probably had to be there.

Hugh Grant

● Taking a break from a golf tournament in October, Hugh Grant went in search of the 19th hole with a group of St Andrew's University girls, ending up back at their student flat. One sexy pile-on later and the pics went up on one of the girls' Facebook pages. From there, they were picked up by gossip Hoover Perez Hilton and were cordially whisked off to the tabloid press, just in time for Hugh's hangover to kick in.

Darren Byfield

● Ex-Millwall striker and current luckiest man on Earth Darren Byfield is engaged to super-polite-yet-sexy pop goddess Jamelia – but tabloid reports of Darren cheating on her nearly cost him his relationship. Worse, while Darren was trying to win back his girl, her fans waged Facebook war on him, launching a group called 'Darren Byfield is a Cad and a Rotter for Cheating on Jamelia'. One of the first people to join? Darren's Millwall teammate, goalie Lenny Pidgeley. Penalty! ■

Gallery animals

Everyone loves a funny picture of an animal. Make your profile even cuter by simply adding fluff, fur, or even scales. Awwwwwwwwwwwwwwwww!

Simon
This is me and a girl I met in Thailand. Things were going OK until this ape-and-snake combo moved in. The monkey had a great night. I got potential snake death!

Phil
I like this picture as it makes me look like a slighty camp supervillain, and that's a look everyone can enjoy

Christine
Here's me! This was taken in 1956 at Peter Pan's Playground in Southend-on-Sea

Lee
Me at Whipsnade Zoo.
We went a bit mental –
hence the hippo silliness

Deborah
It's my favourite photo of me, I was about six.
It was taken on holiday in Devon.
I love it because I was so
happy and excited at
holding the monkeys

Michael
During our honeymoon
we visited Taronga Zoo
in Sydney and got to
feed some of the animals,
including Mandara the
blind giraffe

Greg
Here's me with my friend.
He lets me sit on his
shoulder sometimes

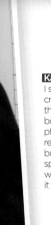

Next Gallery
It's not who you are,
it's where you're at.
Check out our Facebook
globetrotters
p80

Katy
I saw this ladybird
crawling along
the edge of my
book and took a
photograph. I didn't
realise at the time,
but it looks like a car
speeding along a
wall of death. Well,
it does to me!

Face facts

2007 was the year Facebook's network supersized. There's been a 3% growth every week since the start of the year.

"I'm not joining Facebook...
it's full of
Stalkers!"

Many people won't join Facebook because they're afraid of being stalked by school bullies, ex-partners and creepy online admirers. But if you play around with the privacy settings, Facebook is a safe place for anyone

Words **Simon Edwards**

This way

acebook lets you stay in touch with friends and family, alerting them to your latest movements, interests and contacts. This sounds great but, contrary to what you might think, there are people on the internet who don't have your best interests at heart. Maybe you know them; maybe you don't. Either way, Facebook provides a way for people to monitor your life with a fair degree of anonymity.

Luckily, Facebook also provides controls that allow you to restrict access to particularly sensitive information. This means that only your friends can see your birth date, photos and other items that you choose to lock down. Of course, you need to be sensible when choosing exactly what information to publish; do your real friends already know your mobile-phone number and email address? If so, which is likely, why publish these personal details on Facebook? You risk exposing them to strangers, who might attempt to attack your email account, make nuisance calls and cause you all sorts of problems.

But aside from leaving these personal-detail boxes blank, what else can you do to stop Facebook stalkers hassling you online? Follow our advice and leave your worries behind.

One fifth of companies admit using the internet to search for job candidates' Facebook profiles

Privacy tips
Some people believe that, if they've done nothing wrong, then they have nothing to hide. If you share this view, consider the following.

"Who cares what my dog's called?"
When you open a credit-card account, start a new mobile-phone contract or move your electricity billing online, you have to present some personal information to the company so that it can authenticate you later. Traditionally, this would be your date of birth and your mother's maiden name, but now popular alternatives include your favourite food, a pet's name, or even a customised question and answer.

Scan through your Facebook profile and see if you (and, therefore, anyone else) could answer basic questions about you. If so, a potential thief has access to your security answers and it's time to edit your profile and call your bank.

▲ PEOPLE often feel strangely comfortable revealing details online that they would never discuss in 'real life'. But beware!

"Surely my sexuality is no-one else's business?"
Facebook lets you categorise yourself in many ways, including your sexual preference, relationship status and political views. And although this information is deeply personal, posting it on Facebook makes it available to complete strangers or, even worse in some cases, people you know. It's amazing that some people feel comfortable publishing personal information on the internet when they'd shy away from discussing the same details in 'real life'.

Aside from shocking parents and siblings, you might ruin your chances of getting a job. In the UK it's illegal for a company to discriminate against job applicants on the basis of their sexuality, race, age or a number of other attributes. Surveys suggest, however, that employers look up prospective employees using social-networking sites such as Facebook. YouGov – a market-research agency pioneering the use of the internet and information technology to collect data for market research and public consultation – found that a fifth of employers search for candidates' profiles online, and more than half of those claim that what they found affected their decision to employ.

Even if a company is officially committed to equal opportunities, if your listed hobbies or political leanings are at odds with the company's own culture, you might not even make it as far as the interview.

▼ YOU CAN flag up personal relationships with friends, or keep them to yourself

"How could a stalker find me?"

The most disturbing user of personal information is sexually motivated. Your Facebook profile can provide a daily blow-by-blow account of your activities, thoughts and movements. This provides plenty of fuel to stoke the fantasies of others, as well as data that could help a stalker locate a potential victim.

While many social-networking sites insist that users be of adult age, the fact remains that many children use them to stay in touch with their schoolfriends. Indeed, although Facebook discourages under-13s from registering and advises that under-18s ask for parental permission, the fact remains that the site has a lot of young members. By exposing details of their lives, including photos, to the general population, these kids risk attracting the attentions of sexual predators.

▲ YOU MAY get a message from someone with your friend's name, but have you verified it's really them?

The anonymity of the web, combined with easy-to-use community websites like Facebook, means that children can naively leak sensitive personal details, and perverts can pretend to be something other than their real selves. This is a dangerous combination, and there has already been a raft of cases where paedophiles have groomed and made contact with children using social-networking sites.

Being an adult does not make you immune to the unhealthy interests of others. Total strangers can see your photo and read about your interests, while casual acquaintances can delve into your life in a disturbingly uncasual way.

Stalkers don't even have to make an effort, because Facebook's News Feed feature automatically hands information about each user to their friends (who may not be real, close friends). Go through your Friends list and see if you're happy for every

Case study

Even if you discover that one of your Facebook 'friends' is really a nasty piece of work, you might have a job getting rid of them. You could remove them from your list of friends and even block them, which prevents them from searching for you. However, we know of a case where a stalker befriended his victim's friends. When the victim, who we'll

call Miss X, blocked him, he was still able to find out where she was going, with whom and so on. He did this by staying in close contact with her friends, and was able to see details of her life by watching their homepages. These people didn't know him but had assumed he was OK and a 'friend' because he knew Miss X. Eventually, most people realised he was an undesirable individual and they blocked him.

one of those people to know that you are seeing a new boy/girlfriend, exactly what they look like and that you will both be in the local pub this evening.

If you're the sort of person who details these facts and events on your profile, via comments to friends and by writing on people's walls, consider editing your News Feed privacy settings to prevent these things being published to all and sundry. Alternatively, keep your life off Facebook and between you and the people you completely trust.

▲ FRIENDS might think this kind of photo is the funniest thing going, but will prospective employers agree with them?

"What's wrong with my crazy photos?"

Embarrassing photographs can also land you in hot water. Your mates might think that the shot of you

hauling on a foot-long spliff, sat astride a Milton Keynes concrete cow, is the funniest thing since the previous weekend (when you got drunk at a party, fell asleep and everyone drew on your face). They might be right, but making photos of these events publicly available won't impress most employers.

"I often arrange my social life online – is that a mistake?"

To understand the serious risks that stalkers could pose to you, consider the sort of information that someone might need if they wanted to track your movements, either to gain an insight into your daily life or to go one step further and attempt to

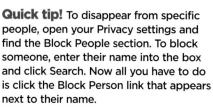

Quick tip! To disappear from specific people, open your Privacy settings and find the Block People section. To block someone, enter their name into the box and click Search. Now all you have to do is click the Block Person link that appears next to their name.

Browse Events Popular Events Export Events

31 Events   Search for Events   + Creat

Upcoming Events **Friends' Events** **Past Events**

Wednesday, October 31

Halloween Party   View E
Because we all should...   Add to
Hosted by:
Type: Party - Cocktail Party
Where: Shunt Vaults
When: Wednesday, October 31 from 7:00 pm to 2:00 am
Friends:

Saturday, November 10

WHITE MISCHIEF: "From The Earth To The Moon"   View E
*Headlined by British Sea Power, a one night festival with 7 bands, 10 Add to
vaudeville acts and DJs over two stages and four rooms*
Hosted by: White Mischief
Type: Music/Arts - Concert
Where: Scala
When: Saturday, November 10 at 8:00 pm until
             Sunday, November 11 at 3:00 pm
Friends:

meet you. For example, Facebook allows you to organise events like parties. You set up the date, time and place and your friends can see what's going on. Sounds good, but did you know that friends of friends can also see the invite?

If a stalker wants to know where their target is during key moments in the social calendar, they can try to befriend the person and track their movements online. If their friendship is rejected, they can call up a list of their victim's online friends using Facebook. If they can then persuade any of those people to accept them as a friend they will gain access to useful information, such as where and when their quarry will be on Friday night. ∎

"Can I trust Facebook?"

Facebook is backed by millions of dollars of investors' money. Last year, three US firms invested $25million in the site, adding to earlier investments of $13million. Maybe these investors believe site users will respond well to online advertising, which is why they want to back a social-networking site used by an educated demographic. Or maybe the data, your very personal data, which is collected by the site, is seen as a valuable commodity in itself.

We'd expect the site's privacy policy to set our minds at rest, however, Facebook explicitly absolves itself in cases where privacy and security settings are bypassed, saying "We are not responsible for circumvention of any privacy settings or security measures contained on the Site."

This policy also admits it stores the email addresses of people who may not even have anything to do with the site, save that their friends invited them to join: "If you choose to use our invitation service to tell a friend about our site, we will ask you for your friend's email address... Your friend may contact us at Info@facebook.com to request that we remove this information from our database." This means you can give Facebook some of your friends' data and, if they object, those friends have to make a special effort to have it removed.

Most scary of all, though, is the implication that, by joining the site, it may decide to collect other data on you without your input. If you found an individual was doing this, the word 'stalker' might occur to you. "Facebook may also collect information about you from other sources, such as newspapers, blogs, instant-messaging services, and other users of the Facebook service..." How easy it would be for you to correct this information, or discover how it is distributed, is not clear.

How to play safe

You need to play with your Facebook settings to control who can see your personal information. Sometimes you might want to provide close friends with lots of detail, but reduce what more casual friends can see. This is important if you accept lots of friends who you don't really know, or you don't verify your friends are who they claim to be.

Below are the most important settings. Click the 'Privacy' button, then go through them by clicking the 'Edit Settings' link next to each one, and adjust the privacy levels until you are comfortable with who can see what.

Profile
● Only your friends can view your profile, unless you've joined a network, in which case everyone in that network may be able to read your personal Facebook homepage. This is one of the most important privacy settings. For maximum security, ensure 'Only my friends' is selected.

Search
● By default, anyone can search for you on Facebook. Choose the 'Only my friends' option to block other people from finding you. People who find you by searching can do things like send you a message, view your friends list and see your picture. Untick these options to prevent stalkers getting into your online life. Essentially, you can become invisible to anyone you don't want to find you.

News Feed and Mini-Feed
● Every move you make will be broadcast to your friends (and their friends) via Facebook's News Feed. Use this setting to disable the publication of comments, Wall posts, Relationship Status and Discussion Board postings.

Poke, Message, and Friend Request
● When you contact other people on Facebook you can choose what information to disclose. Show too little and they may not trust you. Show too much and you could become vulnerable. Choose these settings carefully.

Applications
● This set of options lets you remove applications. You can also apply privacy settings to Photos and Notes.

Don't be afraid to 'ignore'
● One of the most common questions people have is about 'ignoring' friend requests and pokes. If you ignore someone, do they get a message saying, "They don't want to know you, loser"? In reality, if you hit 'Ignore', fear not – the other person will never know.

◀ PRIVACY settings give you control over who sees your profile

◀ YOUR name can be stopped from appearing in search results

◀ KEEP your news and mini-feed to yourself, if you wish

◀ TAKE CARE when setting your 'poke' and 'message' options

◀ EVEN your added apps can have security applied

General Privacy Settings

Profile
What it does: Controls who can see your profile, including your status updates and photos.
Most important setting: It's simply called Profile, and you should set it to 'Only my friends'.

Poke, Message, and Friend Request
What it does: It lets you choose what profile information is shown (temporarily) when you contact a non-friend using a poke, message or friend request.
Most important setting: Contact Info.

Applications
What it does: Alters the privacy settings for your personal applications.
Most important setting: With the Notes application, choose who can see them. The best setting is 'Only me'.

Privacy Overview

Facebook wants you to share your information with exactly the people you want to see it. On this page, you'll find all the controls you need to set who can see your profile and the stuff in it, who can find and contact you on Facebook, and more.

Profile
You are in one network and you can control who can see your profile, contact information, groups, wall, photos, posted items, online status, and status updates.   Edit Settings

Search
You can control who can find you in searches and what appears in your search listing.   Edit Settings

News Feed and Mini-Feed
You can control what actions show up in your Mini-Feed and your friends' News Feeds.   Edit Settings

Poke, Message, and Friend Request
You can select which parts of your profile are visible to people you contact through a poke, message, or friend request.   Edit Settings

Applications
You can edit your privacy for applications you have added to your account, applications that you have used on another website, and other applications built on Facebook Platform.   Edit Settings

Block People
If you block someone, they will not be able to search for you, see your profile, or contact you on Facebook. Any ties you currently have with a person you block will be broken (friendship connections, relationships, etc).

Person: (Search)

Block List
You have not blocked anyone.

Limited Profile
If you want to hide some of the information in your profile from specific people, add them to your limited profile list below.
Edit Settings

Person: (Add)

Limited Profile List
You have not limited profile access to anyone.

Search
What it does: Decides who can search for you on Facebook.
Most important setting: Under the heading called 'What Can People Do With My Search Results' there is a setting called 'View your friend list'. Untick this.

News Feed and Mini-Feed
What it does: Lets everyone monitor your every move.
Most important setting: Untick the option called 'Show times in my Mini-Feed'.

Final Thought...
Don't be scared or put off by all this talk about stalkers and crazies. Facebook is great fun and an excellent way to stay in touch with friends and family, and knowing how to do that in a safe way will only enhance your enjoyment.

What happens when Facebook hits the headlines? p108

Gallery places

Facebook is the perfect place to show places you've discovered. Found a great beach, building, or bar? Make your friends jealous and show them where you've been, in glorious colour.

Mila
I had this one taken especially to brag to my mates that I was in Koh Samui and not Belgrade like them!

Tom
First thing in the morning at Bestival, 2007

Stuart
Taken at Coral Bay, Western Australia, in 2002, shortly before a day of snorkelling

Russell
Taken in 2007 in Long
Beach, California. It's where
My Name Is Earl and *Borat –
The Movie* were filmed

Andrew
Me aboard a Russian
submarine in San Diego

Mark
I was on holiday in Madrid
last year when I spotted
this statue of Tintin

Dom
We were at a beach
party when the
human flame-
thrower appeared.
Stupid and
dangerous but kept
us amused for hours

Eddy
Taken in 2004
at London's
Canary Wharf

Lazar
I don't actually
remember this
photo being taken.
This is my third
cocktail... and it
was still very early

Next
Gallery
Frighten your friends
with a scary profile
picture. See our
favourites on
p90

Create a Facebook event

You've created an online haven and connected with people on your wavelength, but a Facebook group can offer so much more than witty wall comments. Meeting in the 'real world' is only a few clicks away…

Words **Denise Stanborough**   Photos **Joe Plimmer**

This way

Y ou've formed a Facebook group and built up an impressive list of like-minded chums, all making the most of wall postings, picture-sharing and creating a lively discussion board. Finding compatibility online can increase our virtual social life tenfold, but why stop there? It doesn't have to be only on-screen interaction. It's much more fun to move your group out of the confines of a computer network and into the flesh. Facebook allows you to create or promote an event to get your new friends together all under one roof, meaning you can finally meet the real people behind the profiles,

enlarge your social crowd, and have shared experiences to laugh about later. It can only work to make your Facebook group richer.

By keeping relationships purely online you could be missing out on building solid foundations with lifelong friends, or even finding the love of your life. The good news? It's easy to create a group event on Facebook and you can arrange a meet-up quicker than you can type LMAO.

As an example for this book, alternative-lifestyle magazine *Bizarre* arranged a bash for their freaky Facebook friends. This is how they went about it… ■

How to create an event

Bizarre **nailed down a time, date and a venue for their Facebook meet-up, but they just needed to holler from the nearest rooftop and get the message out to their loyal followers. The guide below shows you just how easy it is to create an event invitation. You'll be having face-to-face(book) fun in no time.**

❶ On the right-hand side of your group profile page, you'll find a navigation list. Click on the 'Create Related Event' button.

❷ This next page is where you can fill out the finer details of your event. First up, your event name. Make it clear exactly what's going on – for example, 'Basket Weaving Meet' or 'Karaoke Night'. You can get more clever with the description later.

❸ Next, choose the network that you'll select your invitees from later on. Setting it to 'Global' will mean this event will be visible to everyone on Facebook.

❹ Now you'll be able to input a description for your event. This is where you can really sell it and make people want to be a part of it. Use humour, bribes, and freebies, whatever you have in your box of tricks to get people excited about coming.

5 Put in a time and date along with an approximate end time so guests can plan getting home afterwards. State the venue name and full address, and Facebook will automatically create a map link.

6 As the event creator it's important to put in either your telephone number or email, so people can reach you if they have any additional questions about the event.

7 'Options' allows you to enable guests to bring friends, show the guestlist, allow wall postings and photo uploads to the events page.

8 Now you need to decide how accessible your event will be. An 'open' event means anyone can see the details and add themself to the guestlist. If you select a 'closed' event, uninvited guests will only be able to see the event description and time, and will have to request admission to the group to view the full details. A secret event will be viewable only by those you've invited and will not appear in search results.

9 Click 'Create Event' to finish your event details.

10 The next page allows you to upload a picture to appear on your invitation. Using the browse feature, select a picture from your hard drive that best represents the event. Once the upload is complete, the picture will automatically appear on the page. Click 'continue' to move on.

11 The 'Guest List' page is the final stage to arranging the event. You can invite your whole group by clicking on the 'Invite Members' button on the upper-right side of the page. To individually select the people you want to receive the invite type the person's name into the box in the right-hand menu and Facebook will give you possible name matches from your friends list. You can also run down your friend list and check the box next to each one to add them to the guest list and there is even the option to input email addresses of people who are not available on Facebook. Once you are finished, click the Send Invitation Mails to complete the process of creating your event.

12 Have a great time!

Bizarre Facebook party

When Britain's strangest magazine had a Facebook meet-up, how could we resist going along to see what happened?

The setting for a *Bizarre* magazine Facebook get-together was perfect – a 50s-style diner in the backstreets of Soho. With Elvis blasting in the background and waitresses balancing plates of fries and blueberry pie, an eclectic jumble of Facebook buddies gravitated across London to mingle under one roof and celebrate with their favourite magazine.

The first guests to arrive were a motley crew of Mexican wrestling superstars and weird cabaret girls, who, after a thimbleful of wine, were donning their masks and striking a threatening pose by the jukebox. Also rolling through the doors were a dominatrix, a stuntman, an all-girl rock'n'roll band, a retro-clothes designer and fetish medical models, to name but a few. As the drinks flowed freely and the last of the burger munchers had disappeared into the night, the party really got going, and out came the alcoholic milkshakes. Some loose-tongued revellers revealed their Facebook experiences.

"I recently went to a school reunion set up through Facebook," said a lady dressed as a pirate. "It was so great to see everyone and catch up on each other's lives after so long."

Others talked at length about their favourite Facebook applications and the hundreds of groups they'd joined, from the purely pointless to the worthy causes.

Building a *Bizarre* community on Facebook has meant readers can discuss the magazine and voice opinions on features, but getting the whole gang together enabled *Bizarre* to actually meet their cyber friends and admirers for a beer, after months of only being able to interact online.

Judging by the stuntman setting light to his helmet, the very merry lady doing limbo in a corset and the heavily tattooed girl getting piggybacks from anyone within a 10m radius, the night was a riproaring success! ■

"I like the fact you can check out the parties on offer and see who from Facebook is going, like tonight. I know my status will be 'very hungover again' come tomorrow."

Vivien

"I love the poo application! I've thrown some baby and panda poo at my friends. I have all the zombie and werewolf applications. I also have a pet dragon."

"My status at the moment reads, 'Rhalou is donning hotpants and releasing the Cuban sex badger.' That means I'm going to be a badass tonight baby!

Rhalou

Sakura

This way

"Tonight has been like a high-voltage electric blanket; it was cosy, buzzing and full of lovely livewires. I've made a fair few new Facebook pals from it, and may well meet up with many of them in the flesh again."

Alix

"I've met so many interesting people tonight. I'm actually on Facebook now on my iPhone. I can't leave it alone!"

Mitch

"It's a revelation to meet people you've chatted with online. I'm always pleasantly surprised or disappointed. Most people here have been lovely although some are shorter than I imagined."

Dee

"I spend my time on Facebook stalking boys and un-tagging myself from awful photos. I've had a jolly old time tonight although I've got a back injury from riding a mini motorbike!"

Isla

"I am a social-networking whore so Facebook serves that purpose perfectly. I run the London Vampyre Group on there and we've had lots of great meet-ups."

Darren

"Facebook is much more interactive and fun than other networking sites. I'm a zombie ninja, I'm aiming to become a Bishop in the Church of Zombie. I've met a few other zombies here tonight as well!"

Lue

"I'm really selective about the people I add as my friends; if I don't know you you're not allowed in! This also means I'm more likely to socialise with my kind of crowd."

Samppa

Safety

Meeting new people is exciting, and the increase in social-networking sites such as Facebook means we're more likely to befriend online strangers and hook up in real life. It's always risky to meet anyone you don't know so here's some top tips to make sure you do it safely and still have fun:

Don't go alone
● Consider taking a friend along with you if you are meeting people you don't know for the first time.

Meet in a well-lit, public place
● Choose a place to meet which is easy to find and not too secluded, with a good crowd of people around so you don't feel too isolated.

Tell someone where you are going
● Let a trusted friend or relative know who you are meeting, where and what time you're expected back.

Take your mobile phone
● Make sure you have charged it fully beforehand, as you may need to make an urgent call. It's a good idea to remind people of your mobile number before you go out.

Don't leave your drink unattended
● If you need to go somewhere without your drink, make sure you get someone you trust to watch it until you get back. Leaving it unattended could give someone an opportunity to spike it.

Keep personal information safe
● Don't give your details out to strangers, such as mobile numbers, address or place or work if you are not comfortable. Keep it to email exchanges until you get to know them better.

Getting home
● Arrange for a reliable friend or family member to meet you afterwards or arrange a pick up from a licensed taxi firm. Don't accept any lifts home from people you don't know even if they are a 'friend' on Facebook.

Facebook Groups are a great place to make new friends – p118

Gallery scary

Make a strong statement about who you are with a hairy, scary profile picture. Perfect for keeping unwanted stalkers at bay, too.

David
Meet Dr Blackthorn, my alter ego who only appears at certain burlesque club nights in London, such as Lost Vagueness and Lucha Britannia

Dwayne
A weekend event in Leicester saw me don an *Alien* costume and scare the hell out of little kids, all in the name of charity

90

Ernesto
My girlfriend Julie and I, in Chicago one Halloween

Kindra
I use this as my profile picture because it shows a small portion of what I am about – the occult, dark music and just having fun with photos

Rob
After a summer of non-stop eating, I thought it was time to kickstart a diet... maybe it's gone too far now

Stevie
I'm a massive *Dr Who* fan, so this had to be my profile picture

Michael
Our Halloween party saw the devil walk these lands once again. But in a very James Bond kinda way

Gareth
Here is a picture of me in my native habitat: Evol, the club we ran in Cape Town

Next Gallery
Liven up your love life by posting a super-sexy picture. See the best on
p106

Face facts

One Miami University student was arrested after he set a composite sketch of a rape suspect as his profile picture.

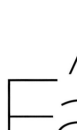

Advanced Facebook

Chatting and posting photos on Facebook is fun, but there are lots more options. Let us help you through uploading videos, customising your profile, using Facebook on your mobile and more, in our guide to the site's advanced features

Words **Alex Watson**

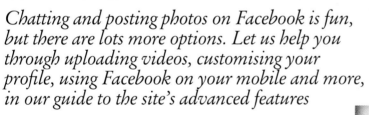

This way

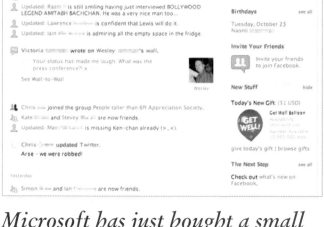

n the week that I'm writing this guide, Microsoft has just bought a tiny portion of Facebook's stock for $250million. If that is a princely sum, then the valuation of the company it implies – at somewhere close to $15billion – is positively imperial. And it's a big empire, too. Facebook's massive value is, in part, due to the way it has expanded beyond its core features of finding and communicating with your friends. Applications, which we've covered in detail (see p42), are part of the reason Facebook is being seen as having so much potential, but the fact the site has many other advanced functions has contributed to its power. Get to grips with these – from customising your profile, to uploading video, and from RSS to using Facebook on your mobile phone – and you'll find you can do a lot with the site, and spend more time on it. In short, it'll seem pretty valuable to you, not just Microsoft.

Rearranging your Facebook furniture

While it's great to be creative with your profile picture, after you've used Facebook for a while you might start to think that many profiles look rather similar to each other. This doesn't need to be the case, however: think of your profile like your front room. Certain elements are essentially fixed – windows, walls, doors – but the only reason the sofa is where it is is… because that's where you put it.

Facebook profiles are split into a series of boxes, a good proportion of which you can move around – although you can't alter the position of your profile picture, 'Mini-Feed' and 'Friends' boxes. Moving elements allows you to prioritise those parts of your profile you use a lot, or think are most important.

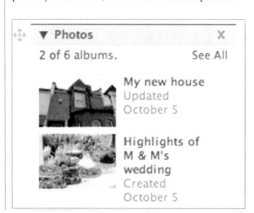

◀ FAVOURITE 'Facebook furniture', or elements of your profile, can be pushed around wherever you want, much like your real sofa

Microsoft has just bought a small share in Facebook, and values the business at a behemoth $15billion

Not only is it useful, it's also a lot easier than carting actual furniture around.

Spotting a box you can move is fairly easy. There's a light-blue header bar running across the top, with its title (such as 'Photos') written inside in darker blue. To move it around, hover your mouse over this header bar, and you'll see the cursor transform into a little hand. Click and hold the mouse button down and you can drag the box around – you'll see it as a ghostly apparition, dutifully following your cursor. You can see where it's going to end up because Facebook places an empty box there with a dotted-blue-line border. Facebook profiles are split into two columns of unequal width – the one on the left is thinner than the central one. If you want to give a box more emphasis, simply put it in the middle, and Facebook will assign it more space. If it's less important, send it leftwards.

Moving a box isn't your only option. Next to the title in the header bar is an arrow, which by default points downwards. Click on the header and the box will disappear, leaving only the header. Visitors to your profile can still see the contents of the box, but they'll need to click on the header to expand it. This is a good way of reducing the space less-critical information takes up – I've minimised the 'Education and Work' box on my profile, for instance – since my Facebook contacts are my close friends, it's all stuff they know and aren't too bothered about.

Some boxes can also be dispensed with entirely. These have an X in the right-hand corner of their header bar. While boxes can be pushed around, reshaped and got rid of, they can't be split up – all your photos are grouped together, for instance, as are your 'Education and Work' details.

Gifts

In February 2007, Facebook added a 'Gift' feature to the site, initially selling them for $1 and giving the proceeds to charity. The initial set of gifts were created by Susan Kare, a designer who worked for Apple in the 1980s and who designed many of the Mac's original icons. The gifts proved popular, so Facebook has kept the programme running, although it now pockets the cash it raises.

Gifts are essentially the third and perhaps most distinctive way of sending messages to your contacts, in addition to the mail system and the wall. If you send a gift, your friend gets a graphic of the gift and a message from you. You can choose to make both, or just one of these, public – in which case it will be displayed on their profile page – or you can make it private and visible only to them.

Facebook offers a huge range of gifts, and introduces new ones regularly – in fact, they'll show up in your News Feed when you first log in, just below where birthdays are listed.

If you click on the gift, you'll be taken to the gift pages, and you'll see the variety of items – ranging from tat to complete tat, with the odd gem – that

▼ GIFTS range from tat to utter tat

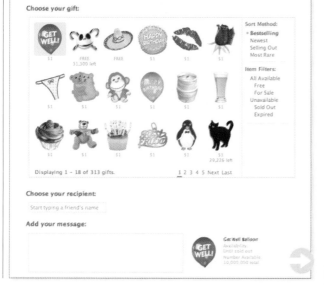

you can send to your friends as gifts. Certain gifts are limited in number, although as they're usually produced in runs of 100,000, 'rarity' is a relative term – you're not talking snow leopards in the wild here. However, if you do want to give your nearest and dearest a gift that's not completely run-of-the-mill, you can sort the gifts by rarity by clicking on the sort methods to the right.

There's also an option on the right-hand side of the page to filter gifts by cost – when you join Facebook, you get one free gift to give. However, there are other conditions in which you can get additional free gifts to give away – but these seem to be quite random, and based on freebies of certain specific gifts.

Once you've selected your gift, just as with the other parts of Facebook's messaging system, there's a box to type in your friend's name, and another box for you to write your message in. Below that are the three delivery options: 'Public', 'Private' and 'Anonymous'. Facebook explains the options very well itself: with a public gift, the gift and the message are visible to all; with private, only the gift shows up in public (not your name and message); and with anonymous, no-one, not even the recipient, gets to see your name.

Cynics might say the last option was custom-made for Valentine's Day. Prove them wrong by buying them an anonymous unicorn in July!

Once this is done, if your gift costs, you'll be taken to the payment page. As with all shopping on the web, before giving your details, check that you've been taken to a secure page – a padlock should be visible in the address bar at the top of

Quick tip! You can give gifts to people who aren't your friends – although only if they've made their profile public. Beneath their picture, click on the 'Send [Name] A Gift' option.

▼ GIFTS COST $1 on the default app, but free gifts are available

your browser, and the page's address will start with https:// rather than http://.

Facebook allows you to save your card and address details if you want, and you can also buy 10 gifts for $5 – half their usual price.

Once the gift is given, you should see a link to your friend's profile so you can look at your gift and bathe in your munificence. Click on each gift to read its associated message.

While Facebook's gifts are a sweet little feature that can come in handy when a mate's had a bad day and possibly birthdays (but probably not for forgotten wedding anniversaries), we'd question whether it's worth paying the $1 charge for them. Sure, it's not much, but if you add the Free Gifts application, you can reduce 'not much' to 'not a single penny'.

Applications

One of the main ways to do more with Facebook is to add 'Applications' to your account. There are thousands of applications available, which we've covered in detail later in the book (see p42), but by default Facebook provides four – 'Photos', which enables you to upload your pictures, 'Events', for planning parties and suchlike, 'Marketplace', for buying and selling, and, of course, 'Groups'.

In our applications section we've looked at a variety of the Facebook additions available from other companies, but Facebook itself has expanded its four core apps with several new programmes of its own. The two most interesting are 'Video' and 'Mobile', which we look at in detail below.

Video

The 'Video' app is a close relative of Facebook's 'Photos' feature, although you need to add 'Video' to your profile before being able to use it – it's not added by default. Click on 'Applications' at the top left of the screen, then the big blue 'Browse More Applications' button, and enter 'Video' in the search box that appears on the right-hand side of

 https://secure.facebook.com/giftshop.php

What type of video does Facebook support?

Facebook's 'Video' app has a Quentin Tarantino-esque geekery when it comes to movie types, being able to cope with a wide variety of formats. It can handle:

- QuickTime Movie (.mov)
- Windows Media Video (.wmv, .asf)
- AVI (.avi)
- MPEG (.mpg, .mpeg)
- MPEG-4 (.mp4, .mpeg4)
- Mobile Video (.3gpp, .3gp, .3g2)
- Matroska (.mkv)
- Flash Player Video (.flv)
- DVD (.vob)
- Ogg Format (.ogm)
- Nullsoft Video (.nsv)

Videos can't be more than 300mb in size, so if you're spending hours and hours editing an HD masterpiece then you might want to keep that in mind – and be prepared to compress it, or chop it up into pieces. It also can't be longer in length than 15 minutes, and must have an aspect ratio (ie, the shape of it) between 9:16 and 16:9. Bear in mind that while you can upload videos of up to 300mb in length, that's going to take a really long time to transfer to Facebook – unless you're borrowing a super-fast work connection...

Face facts

Such is Facebook's popularity, 70% of UK employers are banning or restricting the use of it and similar sites, over fears staff are 'wasting time' on them when they should be working.

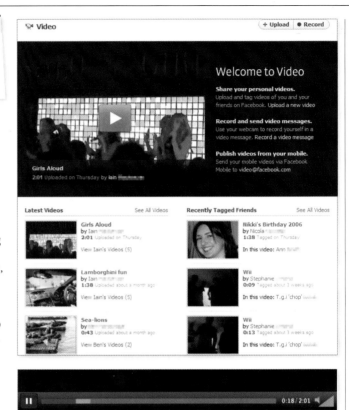

the screen. It'll the be top match, displayed as 'Video By Facebook'. Click the 'Add Application' button at the top right of the screen, and 'Video' will now appear in your applications list on the screen's left side. If you can't see it, click on the little 'More' and it should appear.

Now you've added 'Video' it's time to get in touch with your inner Orson Welles – or just flash your best Beverly Hills smile - and get your moving picture masterpiece up on Facebook. When you first click on the Video link in the left hand column, as with 'Photos' you'll see two columns of videos which have been uploaded by your contacts, as well as videos which have been tagged as having your friends in, from other people. Click on a video and you'll be taken to Facebook's player. It's a cool piece of software – the video is bigger than you see on YouTube, and, as you'd expect, each video gets its own wall so you can leave complimentary comments about the choice of shot and lighting. Or take the mickey, it's up to you. When you click play, there's normally a slight delay before it begins, while your computer transfers the data.

Hover your mouse over the image and the control bar will pop up – you can pause the action, skip ahead if it's getting dull, or tinker with volume settings.

As with many elements of Facebook, the little 'Share' button is also present on the video playback screen. Click on this and you can send a link to the video directly to your contacts, or you can post it to your profile, so that visitors will get a chance to see it. After all, if your friends were happy to be filmed, they'll surely appreciate a little more limelight.

The 'Video' app also allows you to add your own movies to Facebook. You can either send a video file you already have, or, if you've got a webcam, record something new. The two choices are presented as clearly labelled grey buttons at the top right of the 'Video' app's main screen.

Uploading a video is extremely easy. Click the 'Upload' button, and then the 'Browse' button to

▲ PERSONAL and professional videos can be viewed on Facebook Video

locate the file you want to upload. Facebook's 'Video' app can cope with just about any type of computer video, from DVD files to QuickTime, Avis and mobile-phone video (for full details, check the step-by-step guide on p102).

Once you've selected the video, you then get to see the scary and legally binding looking 'Terms of Service'. This is intended to stop people uploading copyrighted video so that Hollywood's lawyers don't come after Facebook. Click 'Agree' and Facebook's computers will start processing your video. Video files tends to be much, much bigger than photos, so be prepared for the upload process to take some time – how much depends on how fast your internet connection is.

Once the video is uploaded, Facebook may have to encode it. Encoding is much like language translation: what you shot on your camcorder

Each video gets its own comments wall, so you can leave charming (or otherwise) remarks for friends

Create a New Video

| File Upload | Mobile Video | Record Video | | Back to My Videos |

Select a video file on your computer.

[_____] Browse...

Please upload a file only if:
- The video is under 300 MB and under 15 minutes.
- The video was made by you or your friends.
- You or one of your friends appears in the video.

Terms of Service

BEFORE SUBMITTING ANY VIDEOS FOR THE FIRST TIME, YOU MUST READ AND AGREE TO THE TERMS OF THIS SUBMISSION AGREEMENT, WHICH APPLIES TO ALL VIDEOS UPLOADED FROM YOUR ACCOUNT AT ANY TIME.

By submitting any videos to Facebook, you hereby agree to be bound by, and that all videos will fully comply with, the Facebook Code of Conduct and Terms of Use. Without limiting the foregoing, you understand that Facebook Video is intended to be used to post and share videos of a personal nature that is (i) of you or your friends, (ii) is taken by you or your friends, or (iii) is original art or animation created by you or your friends. Therefore, you agree not to upload any videos other than original works created by you or your friends.

You further agree not to upload any videos that infringe upon or violate the copyright, trademark, publicity, privacy or other rights of any third party and not to attempt to circumvent any content filtering techniques we may employ.

FAILURE TO ADHERE TO THE CODE OF CONDUCT AND TERMS OF USE MAY RESULT, AMONG OTHER THINGS, IN TERMINATION OF YOUR ACCOUNT AND THE DELETION OF CONTENT THAT YOU HAVE POSTED ON FACEBOOK, WITH OR WITHOUT NOTICE, AS DETERMINED BY FACEBOOK IN ITS SOLE DISCRETION.

I AGREE I have read and agree to all of the terms and conditions above and the Facebook Code of Conduct and Terms of Use.

[Agree] [Do Not Agree]

might not be in the format Facebook can play back, so its servers will convert it so that people on Facebook can watch it. Encoding is usually a fairly harmless process – colour and sound are preserved, although if you've sent Facebook high-quality video, you might see a loss of visual fidelity. Still, Facebook is about convenience rather than image quality, so don't worry about it too much.

You don't need to just sit there staring blankly at the screen while Facebook's little elves are working away on the encoding – it's time to put on your librarian's hat and catalogue all that data.

▲ DON'T BE scared by the terms of service, they're just there to legally cover Facebook

Just as with photos, you can tag the video with the names of your friends who appear in it, and add a title and description. The info screen also has a privacy field with four available options. By default, absolutely everyone can see your uploaded videos. Personally, I'm not that comfortable with my screen presence, so I'd be tempted to go for a more restrictive option, such as 'Only My Friends'.

Once the video is uploaded, it will appear in the 'My Videos' section of the video app, and will be picked up by your friends' news streams. You can, of course, use the 'Share' button to spread the word.

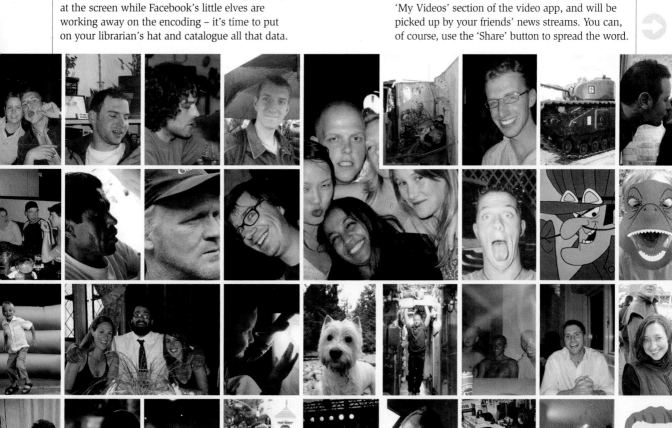

If you want to create a new video, click the 'Record' button at the top right of the main video app screen. You'll see a little box asking you to give permission for Facebook to access your computer's webcam. The small icons along the bottom lip of this box let you tinker with recording options such as microphone settings. The defaults usually work just fine, so we advise leaving them until you've got your first movie recorded. Click on 'Allow', and then 'Close'. The box will disappear and it'll just be you, staring back at... you.

Click the record button and then act as if it's you versus Gwyneth Paltrow for that Oscar. Once you've wrapped filming, click the button below the screen to stop recording. The option to save your footage then appears, but it's probably best to watch it back first. If you're happy with what you see – and lack the budget to hire Martin Scorsese to come in and make it better – then click 'Save'. You'll now be taken to a screen where you can enter information about the video, such as who's featured in it.

You can also upload videos straight from your mobile phone, but first you'll need to activate your phone for use with Facebook – something we'll cover later in this guide.

RSS

Once you've got a group of friends who regularly use Facebook – posting notes, putting up pictures and video, keeping everyone in the know by punching out witty status updates – a visit to the site becomes as integral to your routine as a morning caffeine jolt. The site's ability to create a virtual version of the 'Hey, how's it going?' conversation you have when you actually see your friends is one of the main reasons it's so attractive. Facebook actually provides the means for further integrating this chatter into your online life.

Doing this requires mastering RSS, which is one of the web's most underappreciated technologies. However, it's easier than it looks, and provides a great way of keeping in touch with your Facebook

▲ VIDEOS are easy to upload. Share them with everyone, or keep them between you and your friends

world without having to endlessly check the site.

First off, don't be scared by the abbreviation. RSS stands for Really Simple Syndication, so you don't need to be a computer programmer to use it. It's a technology which allows you to take the content of a website, and re-use it somewhere else. Doesn't exactly sound revolutionary, does it? Well, think of it like this: when you go shopping, it's more than likely that you visit a supermarket, because it combines a huge range of products in one place. It's more convenient than going to a butcher's, a fishmonger's, a greengrocer's and a deli every time you need to get some food. RSS is the internet version of the supermarket. Rather than having to go to all the websites you really love to get your information, RSS enables you to put their updates in one place so you can get to them very conveniently.

RSS is the name for the technology; the place you read the content is called an RSS reader, and the sources are referred to as feeds. With RSS you can set up one page where all the stuff you're really interested in is delivered – and every time new things are posted to these feeds, you'll be notified.

The first step, then, is to get an RSS reader. You can use a software-based reader, but it's far easier to use a web-based one such as Bloglines (Bloglines.com) or Google's Reader (Google.com/reader). Both of these are free.

The first step is to sign up. For this demo, we'll use Google's Reader. If you have a Google account, say for Google Mail, you can log in using those details, otherwise you'll need to create an account with the G-men.

Once you've done this, you need to add a subscription to a feed. Facebook publishes several feeds; the most interesting one is probably your friends' status updates. In Facebook, if you click on 'See All' right next to your status updates on the main page, you'll see the full list of what your friends have been up to. Placed discreetly on the right, you'll see the 'Subscribe To Updates' option, along with the RSS 'radar pulse' logo that you'll see everywhere there's an available feed (although Facebook colours its pulse blue, when it's usually a leery orange).

Click on this. What happens now depends on your web browser. If you're using FireFox or Internet Explorer 7, you should be presented with a choice which says 'Subscribe To This Feed Using…', at which point you can choose Google Reader. If you're using Safari, or an older version of Explorer, what you'll see next will be lots of plain text. What you need is the address – select all the text in the browser's address bar at the top of the screen, and copy it using CTRL + C (or Command + C on a Mac).

Now, switch to Google Reader and click 'Add Subscription'. Google Reader will whirr away and a list of all your friends' status updates will appear.

Any time one of your friends updates their status, Google Reader will be notified. Of course, to make Google Reader truly useful, you'll need to add plenty of other feeds. Most websites will publish RSS feeds – the way to check is at the top of your web browser, in the field where you normally type in addresses, look and see if the radar pulse is there, or there is simply a button saying 'RSS', when you're visiting a site you like. If there is, click on it, and you'll be able to add it to Google Reader.

Status updates isn't the only feed Facebook publishes. You can also subscribe to a feed of your Facebook notifications (when a friend has scrawled on your wall, etc), all of your friends' posted items, or just the posted items from one particular friend.

RSS creates a one-stop-shop, where all your favourites websites come together in a single place

▲ STATUS updates and other Facebook notifications can be sent direct to your mobile

To subscribe to your notifications, click 'Inbox', then 'Notifications'; on the right-hand side of the screen, you'll see Facebook's blue version of the RSS radar pulse, next to 'Your Notifications'. For all your friends' posted items, you need to go to the 'Posted Items' page – the icon should be in your left hand list of applications, or you can do direct to www.facebook.com/posted.php. Again, the blue RSS pulse will be visible on the right of the page. If your fortunate enough to have a particularly witty friend who churns out posted notes of which Oscar Wilde would be proud, you can subscribe to them by going to their profile page, scrolling till you find their posted items and clicking on SEE ALL. The blue RSS pulse will be in its usual position, just waiting for your click. ■

Advanced step-by-step: Facebook on your mobile

Missing Facebook but don't have a computer or internet connection? Don't worry, you can access the world of pokes, walls and status updates on your mobile phone

1 Getting to the browser

If your mobile is a relatively new model – think colour screen and camera – the chances are it has a built-in web browser. If it's a 3G phone, even better, because then you'll be able to browse at a decent speed.

First, you've got to find the web browser, which isn't always easy – the key to access the web browser on my Sony Ericsson K800i is maybe a quarter the width of my little fingernail – but if you don't know, check the manual. What can make matters yet more confusing is the propensity of the networks to give the browser a fancy name, such as Orange World or Vodafone Live.

Once you've loaded up the browser, it will probably take you to the homepage of your network's online offering. This will be stuffed with ringtones, photo downloads and other non-Facebook obstacles – but if it loads, at least you know you're online. Two things to

◀ THE SONY Ericsson's K800i's web browser button is hard to spot – it's about a quarter of the width of a little fingernail!

bear in mind: first, the mobile web is not quick, unless you're on 3G, and on any mobile connection, speed is dependent on location and connection strength. Two bars' signal might be good enough to send texts and chat, but you may find it's not up to Facebook action. Second, although you're sending data, it's still coming – and going – via your mobile account, so make sure you know how much data will cost on your contract.

2 Getting to the Facebook action

Once you're into your browser, the next step is to get to Facebook. There are two choices; the first is to enter Facebook's address directly, the second is to search for the site. Which you choose depends on how easily you can find either option: my phone is Orange, which puts a 'Search' box on the first screen I see, so I searched. As you can see (right), the first result of a search for 'Facebook' is right – "the mobile version of the networking site". If you find it's easier to enter the address, it's:

◀ ONCE you're online, search for 'Facebook' to go to the site

http://m.facebook.com

3 Browsing the mobile site

When the Facebook mobile site first loads, you'll see a small version of the usual Facebook welcome screen. Use the same details you normally do to log in to the site; it can be trickier using a mobile-phone keyboard to type in the email address, and it's usually easier to turn off the predictive-text feature.

Once you've logged in, the first thing you'll see is your own status message, along with a box for updating it. Writing new status messages while out and about is the most logical use for Facebook mobile, given current mobile phones and data speeds, so it's a sensible design choice to prioritise it. Below this box you'll see the three most recent updates from your friends, just as you usually get on the full Facebook site. Scroll down and there's a link to see all of the recent updates, split into pages of 10.

Keep on scrolling down and you'll see all your old favourites from the Facebook site, including pending friend requests, and then a mini-news

feed, with all the usual sections, such as groups and uploaded photos. Any photo that appears in the news feed is a clickable link – and it'll be handily scaled down to actually fit on your phone's screen.

If you keep scrolling all the way to the bottom of the screen, you'll see a series of quick links, to friends' photos, notes, groups, and events. You can also to go to your profile, friend list, inbox or contacts. Contacts is a mobile-only view which lists all your friends and their e-mail addresses so you can easily get in touch with them. There are also shortcuts to these later options – just press the number keys:

0 – **Home**
1 – **Profile**
2 – **Friends**
3 – **Inbox**
4 – **Contacts**

Bear in mind these numerical shortcuts don't work on all phones.

4 Updating the mobile site

In terms of actually updating Facebook through the mobile site, though, you've only got two options: you can change your status (although you can also do this using the Twitter app mentioned on p57), and you can post notes. You can also upload photos and even video direct from your phone, but to do this you need to activate your phone to allow it to send information directly to Facebook.

This process has to be run from a computer connected to the main Facebook.com site; annoyingly, at the time of writing, Facebook only officially supports UK mobiles on the O2 network.

◀ YOU CAN update your status or post notes while on the go

5 Activating Facebook mobile

To activate your phone, go to the 'Mobile' application in your Facebook account, and type in your phone number. Remember to add +44 and drop the first 0.

You'll then be sent an SMS by Facebook with a code. Punch this in and you'll get a cheery confirmation message.

Before we get to the fun, this being Facebook, there's a ton of options to set. Once your phone is activated with Facebook, it will text you notifications of pokes, messages, wall posts and friend requests. You can turn text updates off completely, but fortunately, Facebook provides many ways of modulating the flow of SMS beeps so you don't go completely crazy. For starters, you can choose which events trigger a text,

◀ SETTINGS allow you to dictate how many text updates you will receive

and limit it to just your friends, rather than everyone. You can also tell the system to only send texts between certain hours – so you could opt for lunchtime, after work, or even 10 minutes of early-morning Facebook fun at 6am every morning, should you so desire.

Mobile command centre

▶ DARTH VADER, aka David Prowse, and a fan

- 'srch Darth Vader' – **Search for Darth Vader**
- 'a Darth Vader' – **Add Darth Vader as a friend**
- 'p Darth Vader' – **Poke Darth Vader**
- '@ your last best hope' – **Set your status message to '[Your name] is your last best hope'**
- 'w Darth Vader You're not my father' – **Post 'You're not my father' on Darth Vader's wall**
- 'stat friends' – **Check your friends' most recent status updates**
- 'stat Darth Vader' – **Check Darth Vader's status**
- 'fire Darth Vader' – **Fire Darth Vader**

6 Go mobile

Yes, before you ask, you can poke from your phone. Just text 'p [name]' and send it to 32655 (FBOOK – cunning, eh?). You can also message friends, update your status message, and even search for and add contacts.

Uploading photos or video is simple. Once you've shot your photo or video, create an MMS (aka picture message) on your phone, attach the image, then send it to Mobile@facebook.com. You'll need to have activated your phone via Facebook first. If you want to add a caption to your images, write it in the subject line of the MMS.

7 One more thing

There is one more useful piece of info about Facebook's ' Mobile' application; used within Facebook, it has a 'Phonebook' option, which neatly lists all your contacts and their phone numbers. Click on the 'Mobile' application and the 'Phonebook' link is towards the top of the screen. Handy.

Get a better browser

Mobile-phone internet in the UK is often a disappointing experience; it should be a lot better than it is. While this is partly due to the network infrastructure, it's also in part the fault of the ropey browser software supplied with many phones, and the fact network operators would much prefer you didn't browse the web, but spent all your time and money on their own portals. Browsing the Facebook mobile website using your phone's built-in browser is often only mildly more pleasant than rubbing your eyes after chopping up chillies.

You can get a better experience by downloading another browser, called Opera, for your phone. It's the piece of software used for this guide (and seen in most of the images), and it's quicker at loading mobile pages than most phone browsers. It's also easier to use, as it's been designed by the team who built the desktop Opera browser, so if you're used to Internet Explorer, FireFox, Safari or Opera itself, it'll be very familiar. And finally, it's free.

It comes in two flavours: Opera Mobile is for Nokia S60 and Windows Mobile phones, while Opera Mini is for most other phones. Installation is easy. Go to Opera.com/products/mobile and pick the version that's right for your phone. If you want Opera Mini, the easiest option is to get them to send the SMS link to the download – go to Operamini. com/download/sms, type in your number and they'll send it right to your phone.

Once it's downloaded, save it in your phone's memory, and you'll soon be doing all the stuff you usually do on the web, but on your phone.

Gallery sexy

Fancy finding a soulmate on Facebook? Or maybe just looking to play the field. Why not put your sexiest side forward with a sultry (or saucy!) snap!

Bohdana
I took this photo of my friend when I went to a photoshoot she was doing for a magazine. She looks stunning

Alan
I was at a party in Bangkok and met these girls. Haven't a clue what their names were, though! Damn that bloody Mekong whisky

Terri
I took these pictures on my holiday to Cyprus this year, me and my friend had a bit of a photoshoot, was lots of fun

Alan
It's in stark contrast with the other 'fluffy' profile photos and it grabs your attention. My mother says it captures my tender side

Natalie
This is me dancing on all-fours, round a fire that wouldn't work. Hence the lack of flames!

Jenny
A misspent night in Stringfellows!

Next Gallery
Really grab people's attention with a weird picture. See our favourites on **p116**

Lisa
Black-and-white photos are a must – they ooze glamour!

Tik
This is a shot I took of one of the finalists of a beauty contest in my hometown

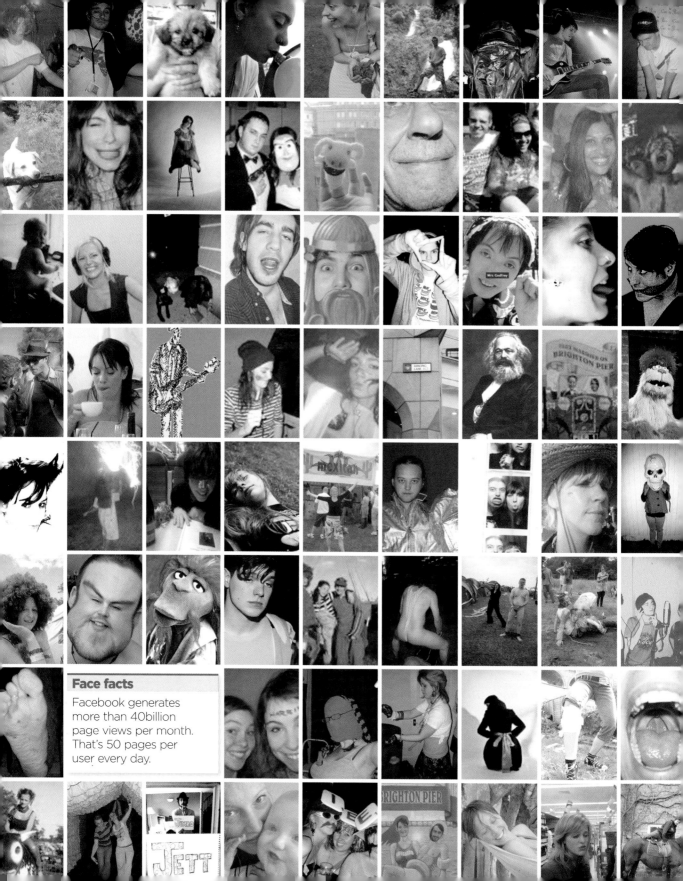

Face facts

Facebook generates more than 40 billion page views per month. That's 50 pages per user every day.

Facebook in the news

It's an information channel, a think tank, the maker and breaker of political reputations, and it's even saved a chocolate bar. The power of Facebook to shape our opinions and lives is phenomenal, and growing by the day

Words **James Doorne**

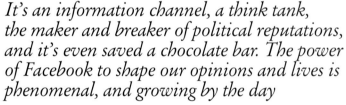

This way

ince its creation three-and-a-half years ago, Facebook has become as much a part of some people's lives as getting up and going to work. And in that time it's hardly been out of the news, whether it's been causing political embarrassment, helping catch criminals, winning fair deals for consumers or helping to bring back one of the nation's favourite chocolate bars. Normally, you'd have to be the first-born offspring of A-list celebrity parents to make this many headlines before your fourth birthday.

One of the harshest Facebook lessons learned the hard way by students across the world is that if you upload party photos to Facebook, they can become evidence to be used against you. It's been a recurring news story over the past three years. In January 2005, three students from Northern Kentucky University were fined $50, given one year's campus probation and made to attend a course on the dangers of binge drinking after university officials saw pictures of them cavorting drunkenly on Facebook.

And students graduating from Oxford University had a similar experience. They had been cautioned beforehand that unruly celebrations would not be tolerated, but despite the warning, some students celebrated a little 'over-enthusiastically', then posted pictures online for their friends, but found to their cost that their friends weren't the only ones looking at them.

Trouble on the campus

In July 2007, the BBC reported that university officials were monitoring pictures posted on students' Facebook pages to see who had broken the rules. The report quoted from the Oxford University Student Union webpage, which warned: "We advise those of you with Facebook accounts to alter your privacy settings on Facebook to prohibit members of staff and faculty from viewing your profile and photographs."

President of the Oxford University Students Union Martin McCluskey was quoted as saying: "It has been brought to the attention of the Student Union that the proctors have been using evidence gathered from Facebook for disciplinary matters."

And it's not only pictures that can land you in trouble. Cameron Walker, a sophomore at Fisher College in Boston, Massachusetts, was expelled after he was found to be "in violation of the Student Guide and Code of Conduct" following comments he made about campus security.

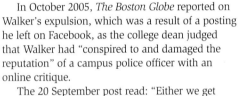

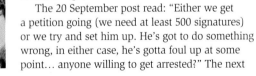

One student was expelled after he wrote a comment on what he thought was a private page

In October 2005, *The Boston Globe* reported on Walker's expulsion, which was a result of a posting he left on Facebook, as the college dean judged that Walker had "conspired to and damaged the reputation" of a campus police officer with an online critique.

The 20 September post read: "Either we get a petition going (we need at least 500 signatures) or we try and set him up. He's got to do something wrong, in either case, he's gotta foul up at some point… anyone willing to get arrested?" The next

UConn hit-and-run probe widens

BY ANDREW STRICKLER | andrew.strickler@newsday.com

VERNON, Conn. - Anthony Alvino and Michele Hall passed each other without a glance in a Connecticut courtroom as they made separate appearances yesterday in connection with the death of one of Hall's college classmates.

Their brief appearances came as a prosecutor in western New York continued to investigate whether Alvino's parents, Anthony and Donna Alvino, of Lindenhurst, tried to cover up their son's alleged role in a fatal hit-and-run at the University of Connecticut last month.

Anthony P. Alvino, 18 of Lindenhurst, who is charged in connection with the fatal hit-and-run death of a University of Connecticut freshman leaves Superior Court in Vernon, Conn. (Newsday / Viorel Florescu / February 27, 2007)

Article tools
- E-mail
- Share
- Print
- Single page view
- Reprints
- Reader feedback

Unruly students' Facebook search

Students at Oxford University are being warned that university authorities are using the Facebook website to gain evidence about unruly post-exam pranks.

The student union has urged students to tighten their security settings on the social networking website, to stop dons viewing their details.

The union said, while it did not condone anti-social behaviour, the privacy of students was paramount.

But the university said there had been complaints about students' behaviour.

On its website, the Oxford University Student Union warns: "We advise those of you with Facebook accounts to alter your privacy settings on Facebook to prohibit members of staff and faculty from viewing your profile and photographs.

"While the Student Union does not condone unruly, violent or disorderly behaviour, we believe that the privacy of our members should be protected and that disciplinary procedures at all levels within the university should be fair and transparent."

President of the Oxford University Students Union, Martin McCluskey, has also e-mailed members to warn that their online community is being spied on.

"It has been brought to the attention of the Student Union that the proctors have been using evidence gathered from Facebook for disciplinary matters," he warns.

Students at Oxford are celebrating the end of exams

▲ FACEBOOK has been making the headlines on a regular basis in 2007

◀ A RECENT tabloid report of one user's Facebook quest to catch a crook

day he posted a follow-up saying that the officer loved to "antagonise" and "needs to be eliminated".

A spokesperson for Facebook confirmed it was the first time a US college had expelled someone for something posted on its site.

In some instances, Facebook was shaping students' lives before they even arrived at college. In October 2007, *USA Today* reported that freshman students' parents were using Facebook to check out their offspring's prospective roommates at college. Any references to behaviour that didn't sound completely conducive to straight As and a job in industry were noted, and parents were secretly asking for their children to be reassigned someone a little more like that student wearing the thick glasses and the cardigan in all his photos.

Magda Manetas of The College of New Jersey in Ewing was quoted as saying, "They were getting an impression – false or accurate – of what the student would be like to live with." She added that "party-related content" was most often the parents' "primary concern".

However, Maureen Wark from Suffolk University in Boston says that sexual orientation is what worries parents most. She remembers taking a call from a parent who claimed to have "psychological and sanitary concerns" about a student's new roommates, who just happened to be gay men. "People don't give other people a chance," she says.

Political disasters

But it's not just students who get themselves into trouble with their unfortunate Facebook postings. Political figures do it as well. In October 2007, the site was the means by which a parliamentary aide exposed his unfortunate sense of humour.

As reported by *The Guardian*, Philip Clarke, a parliamentary aide to the former attorney general Lord Lyell, posted photos of Emma Claire Pentreath, a constituency officer for Hammersmith and Fulham MP Greg Hands, with her face blacked up.

The pictures were accompanied by a caption that read: "Emma's career in politics lies in tatters after she follows Ann Winterton's lead and dresses as a 'Nigger Minstrel'."

Mr Clarke, 24, was quoted as saying that the postings were "not intended to be racist". And he added that he had "behaved very stupidly" and "bitterly regretted" what he'd done.

And Facebook has caused some political embarrassment on the other side of the Atlantic, too. In August 2007, the site was shaping the 2008 presidential election race before it had even begun, when the daughter of Republican nomination hopeful Rudy Giuliani was outed as a supporter of her father's political rival, Barack Obama.

Slate.com reported that Giuliani Jr had signed up to the 'Barack Obama (One Million Strong for Barack)' Facebook group, although she later removed herself from the group and said that her membership had been "an expression of interest in certain principles" rather than an endorsement of any specific candidate.

Mr Giuliani refused to make any comment apart from the Yoda-like: "My daughter I love very much."

However, both those cases pale in significance next to Facebook's most important political intervention, which was during the October 2007 protests against the military regime in Burma, when the internet was transformed into an ideological battleground – and Facebook found itself at the front line.

While the established mass media struggled to report from inside the army-controlled regime, pictures and personal reports posted on Facebook became the unofficial transcript of the unfurling tragedy, and gave people a platform to demonstrate solidarity and support for the monk-led protests.

The BBC reported that a 'Support the Monks' Protest in Burma' group on Facebook had attracted more than 110,000 members in just nine days, and noted that the site "played a crucial role in coaxing information out of the reclusive Southeast Asian nation, where few foreign journalists are permitted to operate and media freedom is severely restricted".

Facebook has also been used to attempt to solve small-scale crime as well. In August 2007, Sky News reported on the case of "The World's Cheekiest Burglar", who stole a laptop, some jewellery, an iPod and a flatscreen TV after conning his way into Jackie McGeown's home in Islington, North London. After pretending to be a neighbour to get past builders who were working outside, and even making them tea and sandwiches, he filled two suitcases with valuables and left, claiming he was going on holiday. One of the builders became suspicious and took a picture of him on his mobile. Jackie then used the picture to start a Facebook group called 'Do You Recognise My Burglar?'

"I use Facebook quite a lot, and I thought it would be a modern way to catch a burglar," she told Sky News. "Maybe he's burgled you. Or maybe you've poked him on Facebook. If you know who he is, let me know!"

And Facebook also helped lead police to the people responsible for killing a US student in a hit-and-run. On 22 January 2007, Carlee Wines, a freshman student at the University of Connecticut, was killed after being hit by a car, which left the scene. It was reported that following the arrests of people suspected of killing her, police revealed Facebook had been an integral part of their investigation.

A 'Support Burmese Monks' group attracted more than 110,000 members in nine days

▲ FRIENDS come in all shapes and sizes on Facebook

▼ BURMA'S monks received strong support on the site

After interviews with suspects who were later charged, police admitted they'd been able to establish a connection between the suspects and the University of Connecticut – something they had both denied. New York paper *Newsday* reported that officers traced one suspect's connection to the university through his entry on Facebook, which listed a student as his girlfriend. He was charged with the hit-and-run and his girlfriend with helping to cover it up.

Chocolate triumph

But before you get the wrong impression, it's not all tragedy and tears when it comes to Facebook in the headlines. In August 2007, the *Evening Standard* reported the case of a Facebook-led Wispa-ing campaign that brought a much-loved chocolate bar back into the lives of the nation.

Cadbury, who withdrew Wispas in 2003, have brought back the bubble-filled bar – the first instance of the company bowing to consumer pressure in their history. More than 14,000 people pledged support for Wispa's return over 93 'bring back Wispa' Facebook groups.

Cadbury spokesman Tony Bilsborough was quoted as saying: "We have been bowled over by the overwhelming online demand to bring back Wispa. The consumer passion has undeniably swayed our opinion."

And that wasn't the only time that Facebook has been used as a platform for disgruntled consumers to make their voice heard. In August 2007, *The Independent* reported the HSBC bank's U-turn over overdraft charges on a particular student account following the support shown for the 'Stop the Great HSBC Graduate Rip-off!!!' Facebook group.

More than 5,000 Facebook users joined the group following HSBC's decision to charge interest on a £1,500 overdraft facility that had previously been offered for free.

The Independent reported that comments posted on the page included: "I am so disgusted with HSBC right now – it actually makes my blood boil. Never before have I lost so much faith in an organisation." Another said: "I think it is absolutely ridiculous. I can't wait to see what HSBC says when everyone waves goodbye and they lose out."

Andy Ripley, head of product development at HSBC, was quoted as saying: "Like any service-oriented business we are not too big to listen to the needs of our customers."

The National Union of Students were quoted as saying that they had "no doubt" the group had tipped the scales in the consumer's favour.

But don't forget, while some users might find it hard to remember what life was like before Facebook came along, chances are your boss doesn't remember its invention with such affection.

Cadbury were "bowled over" by calls on Facebook to bring back their chocolate bar – so they did

▲ ACTRESS Rula Lenska celebrates the return of the Wispa. She starred in one of the original chocolate ads in the 1980s

In September 2007, the *Daily Mail* reported that employment-law firm Peninsula had calculated that every single month UK employees spend 233million man hours on Facebook while they should be working.

The *Mail* said that the study, which was based on data gathered about the Facebook usage of workers at 3,500 UK firms, meant that the total financial cost to UK businesses of their workers "wasting time" on Facebook was more than £130million a day.

The report quoted Mike Huss, director of employment law at Peninsula, as asking: "Why should employers allow their workers to waste two hours a day on Facebook when they are being paid to do a job?"

Good question. Now, get back to work. ■

Polls Apart

Now we know how powerful Facebook can be as a tool in the news, why not find out about how people voice their opinions on Facebook through online polls?

p128

Photos: Rex Features

Want to know how to stay safe on Facebook? p72

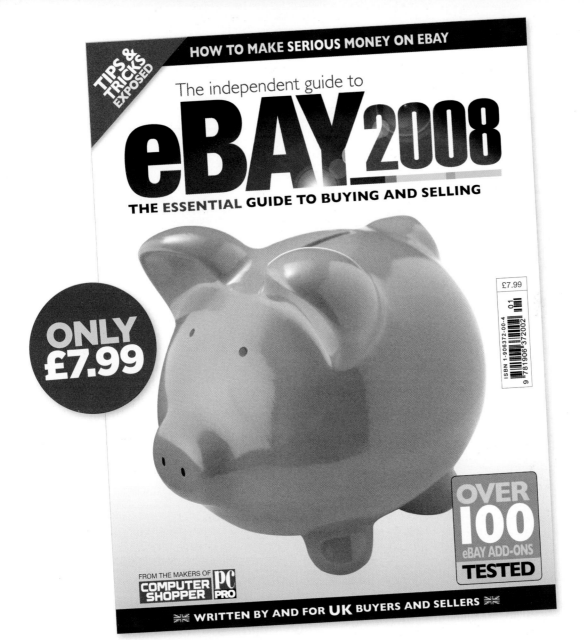

Gallery weird

Facebook has its fair share of freaks and weirdos. And it's a better place for it. Here are our top picks from your craziest profile pictures.

Melina
I won't tell you again, army boy. I wanted a Whippy with a flake... WITH A FLAKE!

Charlotte
I was in a restaurant in Chester with the family, I think I'm blowing out candles on a cake but I'm not sure. I chose this picture for my profile cos it's friggin' hilarious!

Danielle
This was taken for my music – Tiger Lilly – in the woods near Pinewood Studios. I was trying to lick my nose

Richard
Me and my mate Dan – he is smoking a cigar... through my septum piercing

Ian
I was bored one afternoon so I dove into a pile of old hedge trimmings to scrabble about like a hedgehog

Chris
What I hope to look like when I'm 80

Owen
I posed for this picture after having my eyebrows waxed and my hair dyed with a nice blue rinse

Next Gallery
Got ink? Show off your new tattoo to your friends on Facebook
p126

Face facts

London is the largest network, with 1.5million people. Toronto is the second-largest, with nearly 900,000 members.

Facebook groups

Hooking up with your friends through Facebook is only the start - once you join or set up a group, you can start meeting hundreds of like-minded people…

Words **Sharon O'Dea**

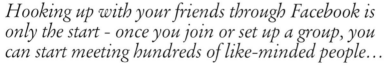

This way

nce you've bulked out your friend list, the next step is to connect with other like-minded people using Facebook's groups. Groups bring together people with a shared interest; each has its own page with a dedicated wall and discussion board, and users can upload photos to the group.

There are thousands of groups on Facebook, and they're as mixed a bag as the people who join them; they can be used for anything from business networking to expressing a love of Kit-Kats. Users can join up to 200 groups at any time, and you can find one on virtually any topic using the 'Search' option or by browsing through the categories on the 'Groups' page.

Groups can be open to members of a particular network only – say, 'London' – or can be 'global', which means members of all networks can join.

There are three types of group, each allowing a different degree of access. 'Open' groups are available for anyone in the network to view or join. If it's a global group, then anyone on Facebook will be able to join the group or read the group's wall and discussion board. To join these groups, simply click the 'Join Group' link on the top-right corner of the screen. 'Closed' groups are also visible to anyone in the network, but only members can view the wall, discussion board and photos. Membership of these groups has to be approved by one of the group administrators; to join a closed group, click on the 'Request To Join Group' link at the top-right of the screen. Finally, there are 'Secret' groups, which are invitation-only. These don't show up in searches, and the name of the group doesn't appear on members' profiles.

Each group will have one or more group administrators. These are the people who are responsible for setting up the group and appointing officers. Officer roles don't have any special privileges, but are featured in a list on the right-hand side of the group page as the group's named contacts.

The most striking feature of Facebook groups compared with groups elsewhere

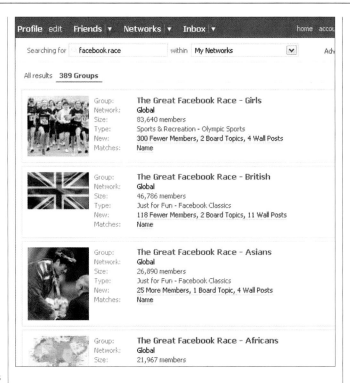

▲ FACEBOOK RACES are hugely popular. Football fans, supporters of political parties and the like compete with rivals to gather members

on the internet is that they're rarely used as a place for discussion or debate, but rather membership is simply a badge to declare that you have an interest in something. Once you've joined, groups require little or no participation, and discussion boards don't attract the level of vitriol (or 'flaming' as it's commonly know on the internet) seen on many other online forums.

Despite this, groups can be a useful tool to rally people in support of a particular cause – group administrators can post events and invite their members along – so they're especially popular with campaign groups, allowing members to share information or express their anger at events.

Conversely, some groups have no content whatsoever, but exist to show that more people like 'X' than 'Y'. The most frequent of these are the 'Great Facebook Race' groups, in which nationalities, political parties, fans of football teams and the like compete with their rivals to see which group can gather the most members. ∎

Groups exist for almost anything, from business networking to declaring your love of Kit-Kats

"How do I start a group?"

Facebook allows you to quickly and easily get a group up and running, complete with a discussion board and photo album. Any Facebook member can start a group on virtually any topic they like, so long as it's not offensive. Here's how to start your own group:

1 From the left-hand column below the 'search' box, click on 'Groups', and then on the 'Create A New Group' link.

2 First, give your group a name. Keep it short and simple, and double-check it to see if it's spelt correctly as you won't be able to change its name later.

3 Now you need to provide some sort of description for your group. This is the information used in searches, so try and be specific.

4 Fill out the City/Town field. This picks a network for your group. You can make your group open only to members of your networks (eg, your region), or to open it to anyone on Facebook, choose 'Global'.

5 Choose your privacy settings. You can opt for your group to be open, closed, or secret.

6 Once you've filled in these settings, click 'Create Group'. Your group will be up and running right away.

7 Now you'll need to choose a photo for your group. If you've uploaded photos to your Facebook profile, you can use one of these, or choose one from your computer by clicking 'browse' and picking one you want.

8 Finally, invite your friends to join your group by selecting them from your list of friends.

Popular groups

Whether it's sex, planets or Dubya, some topics grab people's imaginations and refuse to let go

he left-hand column on the 'Groups' page shows which groups your friends have joined recently. Additionally, joining a group, uploading photos or posting on a group's wall or discussion board can appear in the news feed, and on the mini-feed on your profile. In this way, news of a group's existence can spread quickly across friends and networks. Here are some of the most popular groups on Facebook:

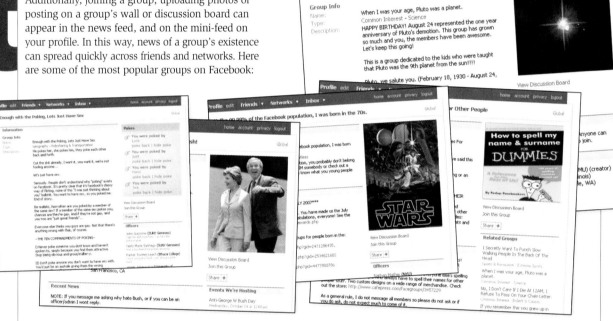

Enough of the poking, let's just have sex
● Members: **291,279**

Although the 'poking' feature is supposedly an easy way to say hi, this group reckon poking has a saucier meaning.

People who always have to spell their names for other people
● Members: **229,972**

Facebook users seem particularly irked by having their names misspelled.

I bet I can't find 1,000,000 people who hate George Bush
● Members: **400,225**

Perhaps not such a tall order in the current political climate, but within weeks of launch this group was nearing half-a-million members.

Unlike 99.99% of the Facebook population, I was born in the 70s
● Members: **115,529**

As Facebook was originally designed for university students, it's no surprise it's dominated by children of the 1980s. This is a group for frustrated 30-somethings to make their mark on Facebook.

When I was your age, Pluto was a planet
● Members: **1,100,761**

In August 2006, the International Astronomical Union declared Pluto a dwarf planet and, at a stroke, reduced the number of planets in our solar system from nine to eight. In response, Steven Klimczak, a high-school student from Texas, started this group, which quickly – and some would say inexplicably – became one of the most popular on the entire site. We obviously love our planets.

Funny groups

What might start as an in-joke between friends can quickly spread throughout your networks to become a global phenomenon

The Derek Zoolander Centre for Kids That Can't Read Good And Want To Learn To Do Other Stuff Good Too
● **Members: 13,513**

For fans of the Ben Stiller movie *Zoolander*. Members are asked to send in photos of themselves doing lead man Derek Zoolander's trademark 'Blue Steel' face. These are rotated each week to become the group's profile picture.

I F**king Hate Bono and His F**king Face
● **Members: 10,355**

A place for people to vent their spleens about the U2 frontman. The group's creator comments, "I hate his band, I hate his smug self-promotion and I hate his f**king face."

The Framley Examiner
● **Members: 288**

Creators of the spoof local paper have brought the format to Facebook, allowing fans to add their own pointless classified ads and news snippets to the group wall.

The Bums Down City Hall
● **Members: 38**

A group in which members post messages as if they were characters in a *Hill Street Blues*-style cop show.

Facebook groups in the news: **David Cameron**

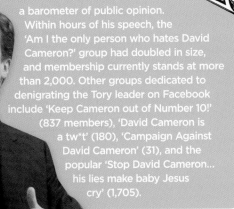

Conservative leader David Cameron revealed his geeky side at his party's annual conference when he admitted he'd looked himself up on Facebook. Acknowledging both sides of the political spectrum, he admitted "There is a network on Facebook called 'David Cameron is a hottie'. It's got 74 members. And I looked a little further and there is another network called 'Am I the only person who doesn't like David Cameron?' and it's got 379 members"

However, Cameron soon regretted drawing attention to Facebook's ability to act as a barometer of public opinion. Within hours of his speech, the 'Am I the only person who hates David Cameron?' group had doubled in size, and membership currently stands at more than 2,000. Other groups dedicated to denigrating the Tory leader on Facebook include 'Keep Cameron out of Number 10!' (837 members), 'David Cameron is a tw*t' (180), 'Campaign Against David Cameron' (31), and the popular 'Stop David Cameron... his lies make baby Jesus cry' (1,705).

Visual groups

Since its launch in 2004, Facebook has quickly become the world's most popular photo-hosting site, and many groups have emerged to bring visual gags to the virtual world stage

Signs that Fascinate and Intrigue
● **Members: 1,389** ● **Photos: 1,076**

A collection of the kind of signs you see when walking to the pub and take a picture of with your phone, thinking, "That will fascinate and intrigue my friends..." and then show to everyone in the pub by passing your phone round the table.

Footballers who look like Dinnerladies
● **Members: 33** ● **Photos: 21**

A group for members to post photos of footballers who have the look of the dinnerlady about them. Members discuss which European footballers would be better suited to a life ladling out custard to children.

Pictorial Entendres
● **Members: 56** ● **Photos: 142**

This group is devoted to finding obscure and convoluted double entendres in picture form.

The Appreciation of Terrible Art
● **Members: 131** ● **Photos: 134**

People who scour the internet for gauche, naive or simply abysmal art to appreciate and discuss. Highlights include a watercolour portrait of a poodle dressed in a Tudor ruff.

Where are they now?
● **Members: 58** ● **Photos: 9**

Pictures of businesses that share their names with ex-stars.

Facebook groups in the news: **The BNP**

Facebook groups are excellent for campaigning – helping to recruit members, share ideas and keep supporters informed. However, these campaigns can sometimes be controversial.

When the right-wing British National Party (BNP) created a group to try to recruit supporters, anti-fascist groups were united in their condemnation.

Critics of the controversial party joined forces, and a number of anti-BNP groups sprang up in response, urging Facebook's management to ban the party. A number of companies quickly withdrew their advertising from Facebook over concerns their brand might be linked with the group. Virgin Media, the mobile and cable firm, said, "We want to advertise on social networks but we have to protect our brand," while bank First Direct said its advertising had to match its "values and identity".

Although the BNP group remains, the anti-fascist groups appear to have won the battle of numbers. At the time of writing, the Unite Against Fascism's 'Get the BNP off Facebook' group had 4,810 members, while the BNP group's membership numbers just 225.

Growing your business

Money, money, money. The smart Facebook user doesn't just use the site for socialising, but also to find business opportunities

Although some employers have banned access to Facebook, increasing numbers of people are using the site as a business-networking tool. Many companies believe that Facebook can add value to their business; more than 6,000 Citigroup employees are now signed up to Facebook, while consulting firm Ernst & Young's network has over 16,000 members. Professional networks can be invaluable to people running small businesses, helping to start and grow relationships with customers and within their industry.

The easiest way to find groups in your industry is by using the search box, or browsing through the groups. Choose 'Business' from the drop-down menu, then choose a sub-category relevant to your line of work. Types of business groups include:

Networking
● **These join people in a particular industry together. Facebook is seen by many as a more convenient way to network than formal events, as it can be done at your leisure.**

Recruitment
● **These bring companies and recruitment consultants together with people looking for work in a specific industry. Jobs can be posted on the group's wall or discussion board.**

Advice Sharing
● **People share knowledge and ask for advice about specialist fields. Particularly useful for those working as freelancers.**

Alternative uses for Facebook groups

Promote a band
● **Musicians increasingly turn to Facebook to expand their fanbases. The band can send messages to their fan group, and set up group events to let them know about upcoming gigs and releases. Fans can also upload photos and videos, and share links with each other.**

Organise industry events
● **Organisers use groups to share information about an industry. The group can then 'host' events (using the**

'events' feature) and promote a series of shows to group members. Once the event is over, members can use the group to post photos or videos of the gathering, or link to blogs they've written about it.

Look for inspiration
● **In one example we found, a budding artist had set up a Facebook group so she can ask her friends for ideas she can work into pictures. Once completed, she's able to post the artwork and video to the group to share with friends.**

Raise money for charity
● **Facebook groups can be useful for getting sponsorship for charity events. If you've signed up to run a marathon, you can keep your friends up-to-date on your fundraising and training regime using a Facebook group. As news of your challenge spreads among friends and colleagues, more people might be encouraged to dig deep and sponsor you.**

Gallery tattoos

Ally
My tattoo is taken partly from a painting by Frida Kahlo called *The Broken Column*, which is one of my favourite works of art

Nathan
I was in Australia, and got a tattoo as a souvenir

Jay
This was taken a while back, and expresses my evilness, and my egocentric nature. It also shows off the tattoos on my wrists nicely

Tarrie
My tattoo symbolises aspects of my life and family! I love 50s rockabilly so I wanted it all in that style

Dave
A freehand tattoo by Pym, based in California. Now I just have to get my leg finished off!

Geno
This is me halfway through a tattoo session. I was having the soles of my feet done

Uthell
8 August 2002, Adelaide, Australia. My birthday present to myself – a nice souvenir from my travels designed by my mate Stu

Next Gallery
Liven up your profile with a sporty picture. Some of the best on...
p134

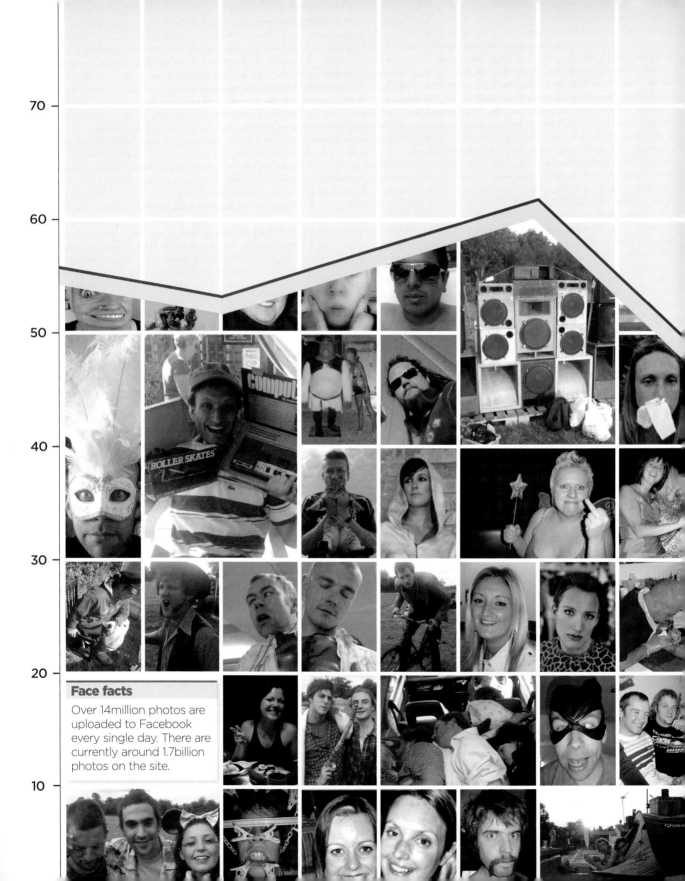

Face facts

Over 14million photos are
uploaded to Facebook
every single day. There are
currently around 1.7billion
photos on the site.

70

60

50

40

30

20

10

What does Facebook teach us?

Every day, Facebook and its users create dozens of polls where users can vote on a range of subjects, from ringpulls to flushing toilets with your feet. And when you see the results, it's clear that Facebook can teach us a lot about ourselves…

Words **Amy Salter**

This way

129

ver had a burning question you never seemed to get an answer to? Well, now you can find out what people *really* think by creating your own Facebook poll.

Facebook allows users to ask questions about anything from politics to porn, and you can then sit back and watch the results as they flow in.

You can poll your friends, and anyone else who happens to pass by, on any subject you choose, so long as it isn't offensive. You can decide how long the poll runs for, monitor the results as they come in, and even display the outcome on your profile.

Polls can be a simple question-and-answer format, or include multimedia functions, such as videos, sounds and images.

Most polls are a bit daft and just for fun – some people even like to poll themselves and ask whether they're 'hot or not'. But polls can be used for more serious questions and market research, and on certain poll applications – there are a few to choose from – you can look at a full breakdown of who voted for what once the poll closes.

Here are a handful of results of polls that have already taken place on Facebook, many of which reveal a lot about the human condition. ■

79%
Percentage of Facebook users who say they log on to the site every day

41%
Number of users who believe Facebook is a healthy way to spend time, as "it's all about the human connections" (aka, pretending you've got 300 friends...)

How to create a poll

Want to know what a random bunch... sorry, representative sample of people think? Then look no further

There are a few poll applications to choose from. To get a full breakdown of results, which you may want if you're doing market research, you'll have to pay for a more advanced application. But if you just want a poll that gives you basic percentages, there are a few free applications and they're all pretty similar...

❶ Type 'Polls' into the search tab on the left-hand side of the screen.

❷ Select the 'Polls' application (or a different one if you prefer) and click on 'Add This Application'.

❸ On the 'Polls' homepage you can view and vote on current polls, or look at archived polls that are categorised by genre. To make your own, click on 'Create A New Poll'.

❹ Type your question into the relevant box and upload any media you want to add.

❺ Enter keywords that describe your poll into the 'Tags' box – this allows people to find your poll in the search engine.

❻ Enter the dates you want the poll to start and end – some people run their polls for years, others for only a few days.

❼ Type in the choice of answers to your question and upload any media you want to add – a lot of polls now have an image with each answer.

❽ Enter your email address if you want to be notified when the poll closes – this is optional.

❾ Select whether you want the poll to be private and for your eyes only, visible just to friends, or accessible by everyone. If you select 'private' you'll have to invite people to vote, as it won't be visible on the polls application.

❿ Select whether or not you want people to be able to comment on your poll. These comments will be listed on the same page as your results and visible to everyone.

⓫ Click on 'Create' to see your poll as it will appear in the application – you now have the chance to edit or publish the poll.

⓬ Once you're satisfied with how your poll looks, click 'Publish' and you're up and running. You can now invite all your friends to vote, and you can publish the poll on your profile by clicking the relevant links on the right-hand side.

35% Voters who believe human beings will eventually become extinct

34% Facebook users who class a mobile phone as the 'can't live without' thing in their life. Friends got a measly 22%. So who are these people calling?

Who is the most dangerous leader?
64% George W Bush
23% Osama Bin Laden
11% Mahmoud Ahmadinejad
0% Kim Jong-Il

100% *Voters who believe the US shouldn't invade countries with nuclear weapons*

% voted		0	10	20	30	40	50	60	70	80	100
42%	Facebook users whose favourite soft drink is Coca-Cola										
14%	Facebook users who make daily wagers with their friends										
23%	Facebook users who can read music										
47%	Users who believe the 80s were more influential to today's music scene than the 90s										
14%	Percentage of voters who agree that morning sex is best										
51%	Facebookers who believe there's no hope for Britney Spears – to them she's doomed, game over										
60%	Facebook voters who believe Frank and Gail Zappa are the celebs with the weirdest-named sprogs, having called them Dweezil, Ahmet Emuukha Rodan, Moon Unit and Diva Muffin										
2%	Facebookers who want more than anything else to become a hero by saving lives										
43%	Percentage of voters who say that love remains, even when the divorce papers are signed and sealed										
9%	Facebook users who hate people eating in the cinema										
2%	Facebook voters who believe George W Bush is as cool as Elvis										
37%	Percentage of Facebook users who say blue is their favourite colour, in what is probably one of the most pointless polls ever										

67% The percentage of Facebookers who say the thing they think about most is – shock! horror! – sex

% voted	0	10	20	30	40	50	60	70	80	90	100

30% Facebook users who voted Liverpool their favourite Premiership club

3% Facebookers who've had more than 70 sexual partners

75% Percentage of female Facebookers who prefer their men brunette instead of blonde

8% Voters who enjoy drunkenly dancing naked on a bed using a hairbrush as a microphone

76% Facebook users who believe if a girl could choose at birth between being a lesbian and a nun, they should go for the former option

17% Facebook users who don't have pets. None. Not even a goldfish

57% Facebook users who voted hamburgers to be their favourite festival fodder

7% Facebook users who turn the ringpull on a can to the right after opening it. Weirdos…

38% Percentage of Facebookers who say pizza is their favourite food

16% Facebook users who believe basketball players are the hottest sportsmen

12% Percentage of Facebook users who say their thoughts are mostly consumed with work

30% Facebook voters who say they'd rather hang out with a girl with no feet or arms than Britney Spears or Michael Jackson

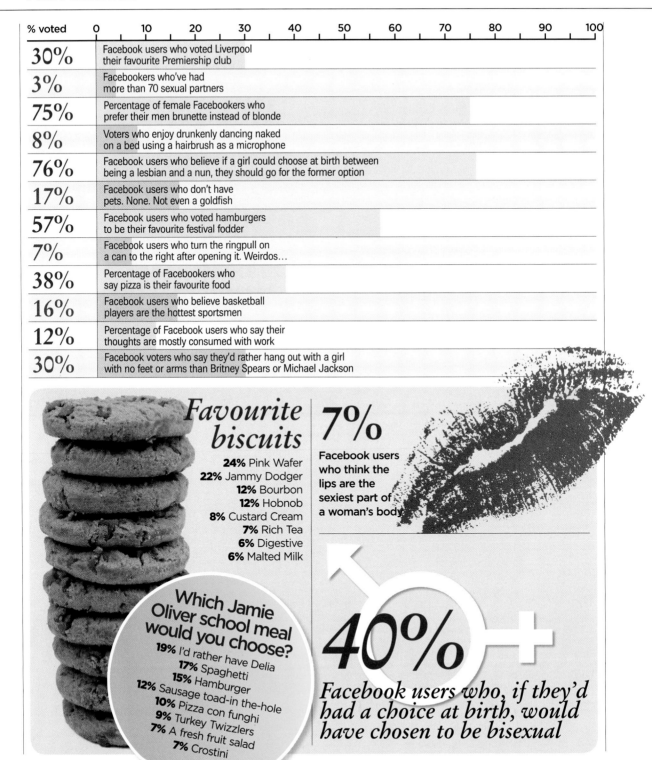

Favourite biscuits

24% Pink Wafer
22% Jammy Dodger
12% Bourbon
12% Hobnob
8% Custard Cream
7% Rich Tea
6% Digestive
6% Malted Milk

7% Facebook users who think the lips are the sexiest part of a woman's body

Which Jamie Oliver school meal would you choose?

19% I'd rather have Delia
17% Spaghetti
15% Hamburger
12% Sausage toad-in the-hole
10% Pizza con funghi
9% Turkey Twizzlers
7% A fresh fruit salad
7% Crostini

40%+ *Facebook users who, if they'd had a choice at birth, would have chosen to be bisexual*

46%
Voters who use soap
to wash their hair

21%
Facebookers who believe
the devil really does look
after his own

27%

Facebook users who believe an open-mic night is the best type of party

% voted		0	10	20	30	40	50	60	70	80	90	100
88%	Facebook members who think girls should have the same opportunities as lads to play football											
61%	Voters who believe women prefer a pretty boy to a fella lacking in confidence											
38%	Germ-fearing Facebook users who flush public toilets with their foot											
34%	Facebook voters who say pornography is OK… sometimes											
39%	Voters who reckon the chicken came before the egg											
1%	Percentage of Facebook users who believe school is the most important thing in life											
25%	Facebook members who think guys really are worth the trouble — but only for the sex											
14%	Voters who say that heavy metal "sucks"											
63%	Percentage of voters who reckon Madonna kicks Kylie's highly-regarded-but-for-other-reasons ass											
5%	Female voters who want a one-night-stand											
34%	Facebook users who say hard rock is their favourite music genre											
12%	Percentage of members who picked winter as their favourite season											

Who's the funniest actor in the world?
29% Adam Sandler
16% Eddie Murphy
21% Jim Carey
8% Mike Myers
24% Other

Gallery ^{sport}

Get fit, have fun, put the pictures up on Facebook. You're a sporty lot, and here are the photos to prove it.

Stuart
A surfing weekend in northern Spain. I'm a longtime bodyboarder but this was my first time surfing. It was great fun but extremely tiring

Eric
Here's me competing in an exhausting, but extremely rewarding, triathalon

Harry
My first time clay-pigeon-shooting at a range in Suffolk – very difficult but turned out I wasn't a bad shot!

Joe
Celtic FC. Seville. 21 May 2003. Uefa Cup Final. We came; we saw; we didn't quite conquer. But 80,000 of us made the trip

Martin
Me nearing the end of a long and tiring race. I think the strain had started to show!

Peter
I'm a big Formula 1 fan, so couldn't pass up this chance to hang out in the pits!

Martin
My extended holiday in British Columbia pinnacled at this particulary scary point!

Harris
This is me flipping the transfer line down at the local dirt jumps

Next Gallery
Travelling the world? Show off your snaps online on Facebook. See our favourites on **p144**

Face facts

There are currently 1.7billion photographs on Facebook. That translates as an average of around 44 per user.

Facebook alternatives

Facebook isn't the only social networking site. Other places offer ways to hook up with friends, meet new people, or share your thoughts and creations. But the one you choose says a lot about you. Read on to find out precisely what…

Words **Sarah Rabia**

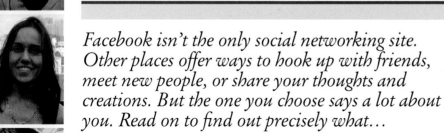

This way

137

MySpace

Facebook's big rival in the social networking world, boasting 200million accounts, is currently the sixth-most-popular website on the internet

■ **Launched:** August 2003 as a division of American internet company eUniverse (now Intermix), who sold it on to media megalith Rupert Murdoch in 2006 for a whopping £330million.

■ **Popularity:** MySpace attracts an astonishing 230,000 new users a day.

■ **Little-known amazing fact:** If MySpace were a country, the number of its 'citizens' mean it would be the 11th-largest in the world, sitting bulkily between Japan and Mexico.

◄ MYSPACE is still holding off Facebook for number-one social networking spot, but these are the two heavy hitters on the scene

Typical user

Over-styled, tech-savvy, precocious teenager who fronts the obligatory local band, called something like The Pallbearers. They describe themselves as Black Rebel Motorcycle Club-meets-The Cure (they worship Robert Smith and 60s garage rock).

The Pallbearers consist of frontman Jack, who is responsible for their MySpace band page, where he spends all his time answering "fanmail". They love MySpace because it has made the band and music their whole life, encouraging them to "think global" and offers the chance of being signed, all for zero cost. They compete with rival bands as to who has the most 'friends' or fans. They're currently at 511 friends (the MySpace user average is 278).

Guitarist Oliver goes to a smart public school with Jack and Millie, their female drummer, whose job is to buy the band's eyeliner and white Rimmel face powder. (And to make the band look cool because it contains a well-endowed female.) They know Rupert, aka 'Lizard', their bassist/manager, from their social circuit – London's Underage Club, and The Griffin in Shoreditch. He's a bit posher than the rest, and recently joined the band by claiming to have an "amazing contact book" - he schools at artsy celebrity Bedales and is second cousin twice removed from Lady Emily Compton, Bryan Ferry's ex.

The Pallbearers all fancy *Popworld*'s Alexa Chung. Apart from Millie, who is only attracted to deceased rockstars, although she did lose her virginity to the drummer in a tabloid-gracing punk band, but it was a "huge mistake". The Pallbearers' next single is a "gruesome ballad" called 'Millie Is A Witch', inspired by Millie's current fad for paganism. The group also publish a poetry fanzine called *The*, which is available in print and on their MySpace blog.

Flickr

The site that lets you share your photos with your friends and family, as well as print them into books, and onto cards or stamps

■ Launched: 2002 by Canadian company Ludicorp, now owned by Yahoo!. Photo-sharing site and online community platform Flickr was originally designed as a tool for Ludicorp's *Game Neverending*, an early massively multiplayer online game (MMOG), but Flickr itself proved to be the better project, and ultimately *Game Neverending* was shelved.

■ Popularity: Flickr is the UK's number-one photo-sharing site. It has more than 775,000 global users and 19.5million photos, with growth at 30% a month. Flickr is blocked in China and many Muslim countries.

■ Little-known amazing fact: Flickr already allows users to print their photos on-demand and publish them as books. In the future, Flickr will add services which allow you to airbrush your photographs, create 360° images by stitching photos together (the CleVR photo website already does this), and, with increasingly sophisticated inbuilt camera technology in mobile phones (Flickr has a partnership with Nokia) and computers, even take your photos for you!

◀ FLICKR soon plans to offer the ability to build 360° images from your photos

Typical user

Annie is a 22-year-old photography student who thinks she's the next Diane Arbus. She carries her Nikon D50 everywhere, taking 'arty' shots of homeless people, pavements and tearful friends. She's "really into" sepia film at the moment – "so undiscovered" – and dreams of having her own darkroom (she has a makeshift one in her parents' shed in Milton Keynes). Annie loves Flickr because she's "not much of a word person" and prefers communicating through images. In fact, she and her best friend Mario, a fellow photography student, from Peru, have taken to communicating exclusively through images taken on cameraphones. Mario just sent through a picture of an ice-cream van, which Annie has interpreted as: "He's in a childlike mood."

Annie has a very low-maintenance style; she wears off-the-shoulder sweaters (inspired by Sheryl Lee's photographer character in *Backbeat*), has a short dirty blonde crop, biker boots, and only wears trousers. Her boyfriend is a photographer too – they're very excited because he just got a quarter of a page in *i-D* magazine shooting a conceptual Glaswegian fashion designer who only works in snakeskin (although unfortunately he could only afford grass snake for his debut collection).

Annie's made "lots of contacts" through Flickr and has had many positive comments on her work (she keeps her portfolio up there hoping Nan Goldin will spot it). As a result, she's been commissioned to take photos of a local band, which she can't wait to upload.

Second Life

The videogame-like virtual world where you really can create an entire alternate existence

Second Life is a 3D online digital world imagined and created by its residents

■ Launched: 2003 by US internet social-research firm Linden Lab. Second Life takes social networking to the next level. Users are represented by an 'avatar', a 3D character, in a videogame-like virtual world.

■ Popularity: Second Life has 2million registered accounts, the majority in Europe, but only 495,000 are active users. This is probably due to the fact that Second Life is too demanding for average users. The hype surrounding it means many brands are creating a presence there, which blurs being on- and offline – users can attend PETA animal-rights protests, shop at American Apparel, and apply for a job at IBM.

■ Little-known amazing fact: Last year, virtual terrorists shot at avatars shopping in American Apparel. Using the scriptability of the store, the culprits were able to propel shoppers out and cause virtual havoc. A group called the 'Second Life Liberation Army' took credit for the attack, saying its aim was to pressure Linden Lab to institute basic rights for Second Life residents. Linden Lab says it welcomes creative dissent and has not sent SLLA to Second Life prison, known as 'The Corn Field'.

◀ SECOND Life allows users to literally build themself a 3D avatar and wander around a virtual world

Typical user

Martin is a 30-something IT support worker who sells avatar genitals on Second Life (avatars are initially asexual and users are required to design and dress them). What started as a perverted hobby has evolved into a secondary income; he earned £500 last month thanks to horny Second Lifers. Martin reads too many cyberpunk novels, enjoys virtual sex with a Finnish woman he 'met' on a dating site, and lives vicariously through Second Life as 'Tyler69' (inspired by Tyler Durden from *Fight Club*, his favourite film).

He really prefers Second Life to real life, as he can be whoever he wants and control his own universe. He hooked up with a Rachel Bilson lookalike at a Jimmy Carr stand-up show in Second Life earlier this year; she would never have given him a second look in the real world. Luckily, Tyler69 is 5,000 times hotter than anaemic Martin Bishop from Didcot and has a much bigger willy.

Inspired by Second Life's first millionaire, Anshe Chung, who made her fortune developing and selling virtual property and converting Linden dollars (the Second Life currency) into real-life American dollars ($1=274 Lindens), he plans to jack in his job and live in Second Life permanently. Martin estimates he only has to sell 3million more virtual genitals to do so.

Friends Reunited

What are your old friends up to now? Find out by searching for them by school

■ **Launched:** 2000 in Barnet by Steve and Julie Pankhurst, who were inspired by wanting to find out what their old schoolfriends were up to. It was bought by ITV in 2005 for a cool £120million.

■ **Popularity:** The website claims to have 18million users, though its popularity is diminishing as users switch to Facebook.

■ **Little-known amazing fact:** Friends Reunited has been used as a name-and-shame board for wives wanting to humiliate their cheating husbands in front of their classmates. The website does, however, make it clear that abusive, libellous or hurtful comments can be removed if a complaint is made.

◄ FRIENDS Reunited was one of the originators of the social networking scene

Typical user

Susie is a mousy late-20s busybody and primary-school teacher, who lives in her suburban hometown with her childhood sweetheart, and now put-upon husband, Wayne. Upon hearing about Friends Reunited over a Rich Tea, she feels compelled to join and tell everyone she went to school with (both primary and secondary, even the one she only went to for four months) that she and Wayne are "expecting". She writes a 1,000-word message informing all of the 'bet you can't believe it news' (she thinks that she was "a bit of a wild one" in her anything-but-wild youth) and happily hands over her £5 for access to everybody's contact details, messaging all 300 of them personally with an invitation to her baby shower.

Susie enjoys aqua-aerobics, Marian Keyes novels and a "cheeky glass of Chardonnay" on Friday lunchtimes with Carol from HR. She has a very thick skin and doesn't feel the need to wear make-up or dress fashionably. "Wayne loves me as I am," she thinks. From now on, any new occurrence in her life, recalled childhood memory or passing thought, and she's logging on to Friends Reunited to share it (they've just got broadband so it's so much quicker and means the in-laws can still get through on the landline). Susie always harboured a crush on Tony, the school pin-up (a short-ass who thought he was the 'Fonz'), now a balding, paunchy phone salesman. What starts with flirty messaging ends up with Susie pushed against a wall in Phones4U Bracknell. Susie lets go before it's too late (it's Wayne she loves!) and terminates her Friends Reunited account... but reopens it after the baby's born.

LinkedIn

Social networking for people who would much rather be in the office or on a business lunch

- Launched: 2003 in California by Dan Nye and former PayPal executives.
- Popularity: 15million users, spanning 150 countries, and site membership is growing by 700,000 new users a month, typically aged between 30 and 55. It is considered the model business-networking site; Facebook for careerists.
- Little-known amazing fact: LinkedIn users include Vint Cerf, co-inventor of the world wide web, Barack Obama, potential future US President, and all of the Fortune 500.

▲ LINKEDIN offers a more private, 'gated-access' approach

Typical user

Thirty-five-year-old Dan is a management consultant and blogger (The Digital Handshake) who lives just outside London (he's just bought his first house). He's slightly trendy (hence the blog) but mainly conservative, and doesn't have time for Facebook. And, to be honest, doesn't really see the point – he's friends with the few he wants to be from university (Business Studies at Bath). LinkedIn sent him two invitations to join, and his trendy advertising friend Joel had hyped it, but he only finally did so after his favourite Silicon Valley-based technology blogger recommended it as a place for people who already have a reputable network, but just want to digitise it and have it all in one place. Now he thinks it's the "Rolodex of the noughties", especially since he's gone freelance and needs to leverage his network and profile. He applauds the site's rules of

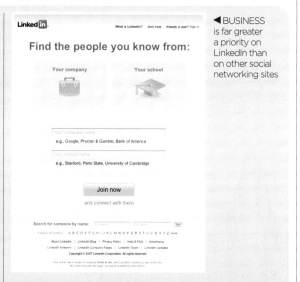

◀ BUSINESS is far greater a priority on LinkedIn than on other social networking sites

etiquette and "gated-access approach" - no pesky emails from graduates wanting work experience or dizzy recruitment girls, not to mention embarrassing drunken photos to corrode his reputation. Instead, business-like introductions and closed networks of like-minded associates for whom the site is about actual work, not play. He's encouraged his distraught female friend in corporate PR to ditch Facebook in favour of LinkedIn to do her business networking, after she drunkenly uploaded a picture of herself mooning in the boss's office for all to see.

Top photo tips and tricks for your Facebook – p32

Six other sites you may (not) want to join

Whether you're diseased, a robot, or even if you're dead, there's a social networking site out there for you

DateMyPet
■ DateMyPet is a dating site where you can check out someone's pet, as well as potential dates for you, and if you like the look of the pet more than the owner, you can set up a 'pet date'. Similar matchmaking sites include Mycatspace.com and Petdating.com.
Datemypet.com

Hdate
■ Hdate is a UK introduction site designed for people with genital herpes to find friends or partners who are similarly diseased until it is safe for them to join the wider dating scene. It has 61,952 members and a 'Herpes Dating Success Stories' section. Hdate's presence shows that there is demand for dating services that are flexible to consumers' changing profiles.
Hdate.co.uk

Book-a-Muslim
■ Denmark's Book-a-Muslim ('Book en Muslim') is a social networking site designed to combat racial tensions by allowing people to book a session with a young Danish Muslim. The meeting takes place either at people's own homes or at their workplaces and is organised through the website. It was created by a group of Muslim academics in the aftermath of the country's cartoon saga (on 30 September 2005, Danish newspaper *Jyllands-Posten* published a series of cartoons, some featuring Muslim prophet Muhammad, leading to racial tensions across the country). Similar schemes are appearing across Europe. A library in Almelo, the Netherlands, runs a rent-a-person scheme in an attempt to broaden the public's horizons. Users can book 45 minutes with a homosexual, an asylum seeker or a disabled person.
Thenetwork.dk/index.php?id=88

Gothicsouls
■ Gothicsouls is a dating and social network site for those looking for a partner or pal who shares their affinity for Marilyn Manson and black nailpolish. Screen names include 'slit-my-wrist'. The site has a facility where you can select a partner based on your nearest Tube line, which explains its popularity with London goths, particularly with the rise of 'Nu Grave' (goth meets Nu Rave) and 'Froth goths' (fashion goths).
Gothicsouls.com

DrugMe
■ DrugMe is a Russian social networking site for people with various illnesses, ranging from cancer to headaches, who are interested in socialising with each other, finding better drugs and doctors, and passing on their recommendations, as well as offering medical news and health success stories. Ironically, in Russian, 'drug' literally means 'friend'. The site expects to have one million users by the end of the year.
Drugme.ru

Independent Robotic Community
■ Independent Robotic Community is a social networking site designed for interaction between humans and robots and for robot-only socialising. Users can use their mobiles as well as the internet to connect to their robot buddies in real-time.
Mediainterventions.net/comunidad

A few more
Ivescrewedup.com: Social network site for sinners; Ourthreads.com: Fashion/clothes-trading community; Grandparents.com: Social networking for silver surfers who want to connect to their grandkids; Mydeathspace.com: Site for the deceased

Gallery travel

Cheaper and quicker than a postcard, you can upload holiday snaps as you tour the world. And make your friends and family green with envy in the process. Happy holidays!

Simon
I was working in India but got a day off to go to the Taj Mahal. Apparently everyone who goes there takes this shot, so I didn't want to, but it came out less cheesy than I thought it would. Just...

Linda
I just happened on this amazing scene in London and couldn't resist snapping a picture

144

Nisha
On holiday in Venice. I use it as my profile picture as it's better than my ugly mug!

Big O
Bungeeeeeeeee!

Andy
Tijuana, Mexico – a crazy place to visit but a great taste of a completely different lifestyle

Lance
Cleopatra's Needle in Paris on a rather long day of sightseeing

Matt
This is the guys and my boat on patrol in Iraq

Colin
Believe it or not, this was work!

145

Jargon Buster

Don't know your poking from your polling? Here's our rundown of the key terms you'll need for Facebook

Application (or app)
■ A game or utility you can add to your Facebook profile

Blog
■ An online journal

Creepers
■ Facebook users who try to 'friend' people they don't know

Developers
■ Computer-programme writers; on Facebook refers to those who write the applications

Events
■ Real-life happenings advertised on Facebook

Friending
■ To add someone to your friends list

Friend request
■ Invitation to add someone to your friends list

Gifts
■ Colourful icons of presents to send to your friends. Your first is free, subsequent gifts cost $1

Ignore
■ If you don't want to be someone's friend, you 'ignore' their friend request

Looking for
■ The part of your profile that tells others what kind of relationships you are looking to make

Marketplace
■ Facebook's classified-advertisement section

Messages
■ A private means of communication between friends on Facebook

News feed
■ A regularly updated list of your friends' activities that appears on your homepage

Notes
■ Messages posted to all of your friends. Facebook's blogging system

Poke
■ An informal way of grabbing another user's attention

Polls
■ Optional questions asked of every user daily to gauge site-wide opinions

Profile
■ Your publicly displayed homepage

Status
■ The area on your profile that tells your friends what you are up to at that instant. Always starts with '[Your name] is...' on Facebook

Requests and notifications
■ Where you'll find what others have asked of you

Social networking
■ Interacting online with other internet users

Video
■ A utility for users to upload video either via their mobile phones or from their computer

Wall
■ The area on your profile where your friends can write public messages

Web 2.0
■ The second generation of web users who interact in online communities like Facebook